PRAISE FOR

good strate-

gies

he nuggets of

bre   you."

                                                 , and

                                                 s to anyone

seel   process."

Pr   lly creative.

ar   innovation

                                                 st Burgers

wi   ! It's loaded

th   nice dash of

"What fun and how very useful to get ideas from such an interesting group of business thinkers. Creativity is an overlooked tool. This book and these people bring it home."
— Jean Craig, *Between Hello and Good-bye*

"A solidly-based collection of techniques addressing one of the most critical managerial challenges today—unleashing creativity in our organizations."
— Dorothy Leonard-Barton, *Wellsprings of Knowledge: Building and Sustaining the Sources of Innovation*

"Creativity is not a secret reserved for a few geniuses. As the author of many books, I am delighted to see how many creative principles can be used in specific fields by different experts."
— Gerald I. Nierenberg, president, The Negotiation Institute, New York City; author of *The Art of Creative Thinking*; and 20 books published in 23 different languages

"I appreciated the book's layout and the inclusion of graphics and diagrams to explain concepts."
— Charles Eason, director, Small Business Development Center, Napa

"I read the book with great interest and found it a rich smorgasbord of stimulants to thinking. It invites one to invent new ways of relating to self, others, and problems—and shows how to do it. A fine collection."
— George M. Prince, Mind-Free Group

BREAK-OUT
CREATIVITY

Bringing Creativity
to the Workplace

Featuring chapters from experts—
Diane L. Alexander • Deanna H. Berg
Bill Blades • Joan E. Cassidy • Rick Crandall
Edward and Monika Lumsdaine
Randall Munson • Jim Pierce • Dorothy A. Sisk

EDITED BY RICK CRANDALL
Illustrations by Monika Chovanec

Sponsored by the
Association for Innovation in Management

The goal of the Association for Innovation in Management is to provide information to help managers and others more effectively use creativity to better fulfill their missions.

Select Press
P.O. Box 37
Corte Madera, CA 94976-0037
(415) 924-1612

Break-Out Creativity: Bringing Creativity to the Workplace/
Rick Crandall (editor)
Illustrations by Monika Chovanec

ISBN 0-9644294-7-0

Printed in the United States of America
10 9 8 7 6 5 4 3 2 1

Contents

Preface   vii

Creativity: Overview and Models

Chapter 1
INTELLECTUAL CAPITAL IS THE FUTURE   1
   Diane L. Alexander

Chapter 2
SHARING OF MENTAL MODELS
Prerequisite for Organizational Innovation   17
   Edward and Monika Lumsdaine

Examples of Creative Methods

Chapter 3
PURPOSEFUL CREATIVITY
The 6 Ps of Creative Problem Solving   35
   Jim Pierce

Chapter 4
HUMOR AS A CREATIVITY TOOL
Laugh Your Way to Creativity   51
   Randall Munson

Chapter 5
BRAINSTORMING   65
   Rick Crandall

Chapter 6
USING VISUAL IMAGERY TO ENHANCE CREATIVITY   83
   Dorothy A. Sisk

Examples of Applying Creativity

Chapter 7
OPEN THE WINDOWS OF YOUR MIND
Use the Power of Reframing to Produce Creative Ideas   103
    Deanne H. Berg

Chapter 8
HOW TO INCREASE YOUR CREATIVE BRAINPOWER   121
    Joan E. Cassidy

Chapter 9
USING CREATIVITY IN THE SALES PROCESS
Step Out of Your Rut and Up to Success   141
    Bill Blades

Index   157

Recommended Readings and Resources   163

Preface

This book will help you and your organization be more creative—and, even more important—innovative. Creativity is the ability to look at your world in new ways. Innovation is the *application* of creativity to produce results.

Results is what this book is all about. Ten experts help you to understand and apply creativity to produce new results.

Creativity is also fun. Opening up the doors of your mind is enjoyable. The format of this book is playful, fun, and easy to read or skim. Turn to any page and you'll see an idea, an example, or a graphic that brings creativity and innovation alive for you right now.

Enjoy yourself. And please let any of the authors know about your new successes and insights.

—Rick Crandall

Chapter 1

INTELLECTUAL CAPITAL IS THE FUTURE

Diane L. Alexander

Diane L. Alexander is president of The MindWorks, Inc., a company dedicated to helping people use more of their brain potential. Ms. Alexander founded the organization in 1986 after being vice president of several national organizations. Her goal is to translate the latest scientific research about the brain into practical and easy-to-learn techniques. Based on this research, The MindWorks' programs provide tools and techniques to increase productivity by enabling individuals to use their mental hardware and software more effectively.

Her organization has worked with corporations, schools, and government agencies including AT&T, Bank One, Honda of America, The Limited, the San Diego County-wide School System, and U.S. Health Corp. Extensive research conducted with the University of San Diego and Ohio State University found that participants save an average of one to two work days per week by using the tools and techniques provided by the company's programs.

Ms. Alexander has been lecturing, writing, and teaching for over 25 years. She has a degree in education, a master's in psychology, an MBA, and extensive postgraduate work in the field of neuroscience. She has been interviewed by numerous TV, radio, and national magazines.

Diane L. Alexander, The MindWorks, Inc., 8480 Davington Dr., Dublin, OH 43017; phone (614) 793-9730; fax (614) 793-1530; e-mail dalexander@themindworks.com.

Chapter 1

INTELLECTUAL CAPITAL IS THE FUTURE

Diane L. Alexander

"Management means, in the last analysis, the
substitution of thought for brawn and muscle."

—Peter Drucker

Brainpower and creativity are the currency of
today's Knowledge Age. Smart companies understand that the key to inventing, developing, and
marketing new products is the brain that every
employee brings to work.

Learning how to increase intellectual capital
is paramount in order for you and your organization to be successful as we move into the twenty-first
century. This chapter will show how intellectual
capital impacts the bottom line. Subsequent chapters will provide you with a treasure chest of tools
and techniques for developing this powerful resource in your organization.

INTELLECTUAL CAPITAL: WHAT IS IT?

In *Intellectual Capital*, author Thomas Stewart states that, "Intellectual capital is the sum of everything everybody in the company knows that gives it a competitive edge."

To visualize intellectual capital, imagine a lawyer in her office. Her office is complete with a desk, chair, computer, books and other general office items considered to be the "capital" of her organization. Yet, it is the knowledge, information, and experience that the lawyer brings to the firm that is used to create the organization's wealth.

Her office equipment is merely an aid for assembling and integrating her knowledge. Her value to the organization isn't in the number of words she produces for her closing argument, but rather the effectiveness of her argument for her clients. Her knowledge and experience are the raw materials that she will translate into economic dollars. It is her brainpower that clients are willing to pay $200 an hour for, not the office trappings.

Dentists and accountants "upgrade" their skills through workshops on new techniques. New drills or computers are secondary. Today, knowledge, not more or bigger equipment, creates your competitive edge. Knowledge has moved from a supportive role in organizations to the starring role.

Investing in Intellectual Capital

Investment in employees produces almost three times the productivity as investment in equipment. The National Center on the Educational Quality of the Workforce (EQW) reported in 1995 that a 10% increase in the educational level of workers produced a productivity gain of 8.6%, while a 10% increase in the value of capital equipment only produced a productivity gain of 3.4%.

Capital Equipment: 3.4%
Education: 8.6%

FROM BRAWN TO BRAINS

From the beginning of the Industrial Revolution until the 1950s, equipment and muscle power produced the revenue. A hundred years ago, a company's value was determined by its capital equipment and value of the land it owned. Labor was cheap and easily replaceable.

When Henry Ford institutionalized the assembly line, he made people interchangeable. Work was designed so that people could be replaced without negatively impacting production. The worker became a cog in the machine.

"Light" Power

Economic power today no longer has "weight" like steel or coal. It is a product of the human mind rather than of the earth and blast furnace.

—*Forbes* magazine

Companies produced mass quantities of hard, durable goods. They operated in a formal, top-down, authoritarian manner with the "boss" in control of all information. Examples of industries that flourished during that period were steel, meat packing, and machine tool manufacturing.

Brainpower Rules

Today, intellectual capital has replaced hard assets (equipment and muscle power) as the most valuable resource for market viability. Intellectual capital is more than research development. It is the brainpower of everyone in the organization.

Here's an example that illustrates the value of using employees' brainpower. A country club health center supplied free shampoo for its patrons. But patrons were taking the shampoo home with them. Bottles had to be replaced every day and patrons complained when a bottle wasn't available when they needed one. Management held a big meeting to try to solve this problem. They initially considered installing signs that would say, "Don't take the shampoo. It's your club. It costs you money." They also considered installing security cameras in the locker room. Before they acted, they fortunately decided to ask the locker room attendant for his input. He said, "No problem—let's just remove the caps from the bottles!"

A New Economy

A dramatic illustration of the brainpower shift is the fact that two-thirds of the companies listed on the first Fortune 500 list are no longer on the list today, some forty years later. The former giants on the business landscape were Sears, IBM, and GM. In 1985, IBM had over 400,000 employees and $6 billion in profits. Eight years later, a third of its employees were gone, and so were its profits. The new winners are companies that have invested in knowledge.

3M is an example of a company that made the shift from valuing hard assets to valuing knowledge. Originally known as Minnesota Mining and Manufacturing, the company dealt in "hard" assets. Long since redefined as "3M," their core competencies now are knowledge of materials like adhesives, and the creativity of their employees.

It's no accident that 3M produces hundreds of new products a year. Employees are allowed to spend 10% of their time developing ideas that have been turned down by the company. And when successful, they can receive 1% of the profits on a new product they develop. The inventor of Post-It® Notes gets $1 million a year.

Don't Fear Failure

IBM was more concerned with avoiding errors than with encouraging people to take intelligent risks. Encourage fresh ideas. IBM believed in their own infallibility, so they discouraged novel approaches.

—Professor Eugene Jennings, Michigan State University

"The only way to encourage creativity is to make it clear that failure is not the ultimate mistake. There is a problem only when you fail in the same way more than once."

—George Rathmann, former CEO of Amgen, Inc. (a biotech company)

FROM SMOKE STACKS TO MICROCHIPS: VALUING INTELLECTUAL CAPITAL IN THE KNOWLEDGE ECONOMY

Investors don't buy Microsoft stock because of its factories and heavy equipment. It doesn't own any. People invest because of the marketing

The New Source of Wealth

"Information is the new source of wealth. But unless business can measure the intangible assets that constitute intellectual capital—which creates valuable information, productivity, and success—wealth cannot be expected or assured."

—Michael Malone, co-author, *Intellectual Capital: Realizing Your Company's True Value by Finding Its Hidden Brainpower*

Balance Sheet	
HARD ASSETS	BRAIN ASSETS
• plant	• employee skills
• equipment	• patents
• land	• processes
• inventory	• customer relationships

acumen of Bill Gates and all of the people behind him who write code, anticipate the software market, and form business alliances.

The value of intellectual capital can be estimated through the stock market. In the past, a company's worth was determined by valuing its land, buildings, and equipment—book value. Today, however, many stocks sell at 3–10 times the book value of their assets. This indicates that stockholders place a value on the potential of the individuals, the systems, and the relationships with customers and believe that these knowledge-based assets will contribute to the long-term profitability of the company.

Examples of Brainpower at Work

This increasing emphasis on brainpower doesn't mean that hard goods will no longer be produced. It means that new goods will be developed through innovation, and that the goods will be produced more efficiently.

For instance, Reynolds Metal invented a way to mass produce aluminum cans that were half the weight of standard steel cans. As a result, they were able to capture 99 percent of the lucrative U.S. beverage steel can business and are now in the process of doing the same on a global scale.

Netscape Communications is a relatively new company. Unlike Reynolds Metal, it has a low asset base. In fact, it doesn't even produce a tangible product—its Navigator software gets into your computer via modem straight from the Netscape servers. Yet after only three years of operation, its stock was valued at nearly a billion dollars!

InterDesign, a $20-million company located outside Cleveland, sells plastic products such as wastepaper baskets and soap dishes. These products are far from the high-tech world. But InterDesign has used computers to change the way it does business. An employee used to drive to the post office everyday to pick up orders that were then processed by hand. As a result of the manual processing, errors often occurred in filling the orders, and little information about customers' selection of products was easily available to the marketing department.

Sharing Ideas Widely

To keep good ideas from being lost at Wabash National Corporation's truck trailer assembly plant, individuals or teams that come up with innovative solutions enter their techniques into a database. The database is available company-wide through a local-area network. This both preserves the idea and makes new information readily available to others.

—*Executive Edge* newsletter

Today, the megabytes of computer power are up thirtyfold at InterDesign. Orders arrive straight into the company's computers from customers. They are filled with near-perfect accuracy. The computer allows the marketing department almost immediate access to data about customer product selection, color, and quantity. This information has enabled InterDesign to become a leading product innovator in its field.

Business Intellectual Capital

What do all of these companies have in common? Certainly not the products they produce, nor their customer base, nor their length of time in business. They all have achieved success in their respective industries by emphasizing knowledge over the traditional resources of money and capital equipment. Each of these companies has targeted intellectual capital and made it their most important factor of production.

As a result, they have succeeded in:
- freeing up other capital
- attracting talented people
- creating a competitive edge
- enjoying unprecedented growth and sustainability

MANAGING BRAINPOWER FOR INNOVATION

The Knowledge Age hasn't ended our need for goods and services. But it has changed how these goods are made, marketed, and distributed. And it is this change that is requiring new skills from employees, new work methods and processes, and new ways of managing.

Successful organizations are structured around participative teams that can be highly mobile and responsive to dynamic environments. This structure requires the sharing of information throughout the organization and employee empowerment and involvement at all levels.

The Creativity Paradox

"Individual, corporate, and economic progress turn on a paradox: We are entering the age of value added through knowledge. Yet the very tools that carry us along this path seem to...shut down the curiosity and creativity that's needed now more than ever."

—Tom Peters

Ask for Input

Huber's Engineered Carbons Division launched its Quality Management System in 1978. The division had lost 40% of its market share and was looking for a way to turn things around.

They wanted to involve employees as quickly as possible, so they started suggestion contests. In one division, as long as an idea had some merit, it was put in a raffle for a pickup truck. Another plant gave a $1,000 savings bond to the employee whose suggestion produced the most savings.

At first, there was a shortage of suggestions, so they started a Write Improvement Proposals Everyday (WIPE) and paid $1 per idea. A manager recalled, "These incentives were like spreading fertilizer on a field. Ideas started popping up everywhere...We used to just get employees' backs, now we're getting their minds, too."

A plant manager said, "Amazing things happen when you give people more responsibility. One of our hourly maintenance guys cut seven hours off the amount of time it takes to re-bag our equipment filers. Our sieve residue, which is one of our best indicators of product quality, used to be 200 parts per million. Now, as a result of little improvements, it's down to five parts per million."

Using Your Brains

In recent research by the Gottlieb Duttweiler Foundation, a Swiss think tank, CEOs estimated that only 20 percent of their companies' available knowledge was actually used. Imagine if factories, machinery, and offices were only utilized 20 percent of the time? The loss of potential revenue would be staggering.

The loss of potential revenue from not developing the brain power of an organization is equally staggering. The human brain is still the most powerful piece of "equipment" in the office or factory. Understanding how to encourage innovation so that new ideas are produced to increase profits and reduce expenditures should be the focus of each manager and employee.

Jack Welch, GE's chairman, attributes their continual 6–7 percent productivity increases to the ideas that employees bring to the job. These ideas produce value-added enhancements, reduce costly production errors, and build strong customer loyalty. Thus they increase productivity for the organization. Providing the

---

How to Get Employees to Share Ideas

The key to generating good ideas lies in better internal communication.

(1) Make sure the employees receive timely, reliable information about where the company is heading, and what the problems are and will be. Let them know that management wants their help.

(2) Ask each employee to jot down the one or two things the supervisor can do to help get the job done better.

(3) Conduct working smarter vs. working harder sessions with all employees. Ask them to comment on how they might generate higher productivity.

—*Communications Briefings* newsletter

Reward Bright Ideas

To persuade people to make more suggestions, make sure they know that you consider all of their ideas. Drive your message home by presenting each person with a notebook embossed with the company logo, plus a calculator and a pen and pencil set. Title the notebook the "Bright Ideas Notebook" and inscribe it with this message: "We need and want your ideas! When you get an idea, write it down and submit it."

—Michael Michalko, *Thinkertoys*

thinking tools and techniques to enable employees to be innovative in their approaches to their jobs allows the company to remain competitively alive.

Valuing Innovation and Brains

Today's knowledge workers are valuable because of what they know and the kinds of solutions they can develop. The more an employee learns, creates and implements, the more valuable he or she is.

In a company that values knowledge, the primary purpose of a worker is not to be a cog in the wheel, but to be an inventor of new products, an improver of efficiency, and a builder of customer relations. The more effective the employee is at these skills, the more viable is the company. Employee brains are the store of value.

Let's take a look at how this change in employee roles is impacting companies.

This change in the typical worker can be seen in real life at Corning which has long been a major producer of durable goods. Two-thirds of its employees used their "hands" to work on "things" in 1972. Manual labor produced revenue.

Today, robots have replaced much of the manual labor. The result at Corning is that two-thirds of their employees use their minds to work with ideas, concepts, and information. Employees have moved from muscle power to brainpower to create products for the market.

Employee Suggestions

In one year, Toyota employees submitted 860,000 suggestions for improvement. Sixty-six percent of employees in Japan regularly generate ideas. Only 8% of American employees do. One reason may be that, on average, Japanese managers use four out of five suggestions, and American managers only use one in four.

66%

8%

U.S.   Japan

Collaboration Fosters Creativity

If you ask, "What happened here?" when a problem occurs, you'll get observations. Get creative ideas to a problem by asking, "How to you think we can fix the problem so it won't happen again." You'll hear ideas that you never thought of before.

—*Managing Beyond the Ordinary* by Charles H. Keener and Hirotsugu Iikubo

BRAIN 101: HOW THE BRAIN WORKS

Let's take a look at how your three-pound portable "think tank" works and how you can tap into more of its vast potential.

The brain is composed of two muscles that have a connective bridge between the two. The two muscles are able to pass electrical impulses back and forth across this connective bridge called the corpus callosum. A grand mal seizure is a muscle spasm that occurs in one muscle of the brain and passes over to the other muscle causing it to go into spasm. During World War II, an American soldier in a German POW camp was hit in the head with the butt of a rifle. The blow was so intense that it caused him to begin having epiletic seizures. By the time he returned to the states, he was having about 100 grand seizures a day.

Unable to provide this soldier with any relief, doctors decided to sever the corpus callosum. As a result, when one muscle of the brain would go into spasm it could not pass the spasm over to the other muscle. By containing the spasm, doctors were able to treat the localized seizure with medication. This radical procedure provided the man with relief from his seizures and enabled him to live a more normal life.

Doctors then began treating other epileptic patients in this manner.

As an accidental benefit, doctors had a unique group of patients on whom they could do tests of brain "localization."

In 1981, Dr. Roger Sperry won the Nobel Prize in medicine for his "split brain theory." Through his research, he found that each section of the brain had its own area of specialty.

Today, we know that the brain is enormously com-

Brain Functions

LEFT BRAIN	RIGHT BRAIN
• verbal	• new ideas/ creative
• analytical	• musical/artistic
• literal	• spacial
• linear	• nonverbal
• mathematical	• metaphoric
• sequential	• playful
• concrete	• emotional
• rational	• spontaneous
• skeptical	• intuitive
• closed	• symbolic
• cautious	• work with people
• work with things	

plex, but Sperry's theory provides a helpful metaphor for how the brain works. Sperry stated that the left side of the brain is responsible for logic, data, numbers, planning, organizing, following orders, and working with things. The right side is responsible for looking at the big picture; innovation, managing change, taking risks, relying on hunches, and relationship building.

APPLIED BRAIN 201

The brain is a muscle that can be exercised. Which side of your brain was exercised while you were growing up?

School prepared us to have the skills and resources needed for the Industrial Age. If you were like most students, you spent time sitting in rows, memorizing data from a book, and coloring in between the lines. All of these activities tend to engage more of the left brain. Thus the left muscle was built up, enabling us to get jobs that required us to follow directions, sit at our desks, and work quietly.

Then came the Information Age and the restructuring of organizations and work. Now managers are asking employees to move from a highly stable environment to one that embraces change.

Instead of following the standard procedures, employees are suddenly being asked to develop innovative solutions to problems. Instead of working alone, em-

---

Lively Fish

One way to exercise your creativity is to subdivide a challenge into parts. These parts can give you new ideas. For instance, a frozen-fish processor found that dead or listless fish awaiting processing tasted bland. Even keeping the fish alive in tanks didn't help. He listed the attributes of what made a fish a fish:

- lives underwater
- has gills and fins
- cold-blooded
- constantly moves to avoid predators
- changes color out of water

Looking at the separate parts, he came up with a solution. He put a small shark in the tank with the fish. The fish kept moving to avoid the shark and the fresh flavor returned.

—Michael Michalko, *Thinkertoys*

ployees are expected to work in cross-functional teams in a collaborative manner.

Not only have the rules of the game been changed, but we're now asking people to operate more from their creative right brains—generally the less developed side. And organizations wonder why employees seem to have a hard time adjusting to the new expectations!

The critical question becomes, what can be done to exercise those parts of the brain that are so desperately needed by organizations? Let's take a look at how the brain can be exercised to produce these new areas of success.

Enhancing Brainpower: Sink or Swim!

Researcher Marian Diamond, at the University of California at Berkeley, conducted experiments with mice in an effort to identify those factors that were critical to brainpower. In her experiments, she randomly raised mice in one of three cages. Mice in the first cage were placed alone in their cages. The second cage housed two mice but no toys. The third cage held up to twelve mice, and contained many toys.

After a period of time in their cages, the mice were placed in a large barrel filled with water with an island in the center. The mice from the first two cages always drowned when placed in the barrel of water. However, when the mice from the third cage were placed in the barrel of water, they always figured out how to swim to the island and, therefore, survived. The important question was what was impacting the brainpower of the mice and enabling one group to consistently succeed over the other two groups.

It was found that the brains of each group had developed physically differently as a result of the activities they experienced in their environments. The mice in the enriched environment had exercised their brain muscles differently.

Brain cells are composed of two main components—the cell body and dendrites/axons. The dendrites/axons can be significantly impacted by environmental stimulation. A thought or idea is primarily an electrical connection between a dendrite and an axon. The box at left portrays a brain cell from a normal mouse and a brain cell from a mouse in the enriched cage.

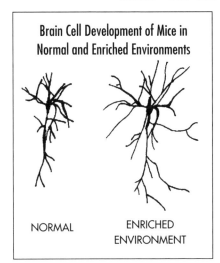

Brain Cell Development of Mice in Normal and Enriched Environments

NORMAL   ENRICHED ENVIRONMENT

The enriched environment stimulated brain cell development. This group had grown more dendrites from their mental exercising. They, therefore, had the physical resources available to make new connections when they had to problem-solve (getting to the island). The mice in the other two cages were not able to develop new ideas because they had not developed the necessary connective tissue.

COMPANY CREATIVITY

Creativity is analogous to brain dendrites. Creativity is the ability to make connections that others haven't. Companies that foster creativity, encourage connections within the company, and within the individual. This produces the ability to make more responses faster, which ultimately produces more innovation and better solutions. The bad news is that creative success is dependent on new skills and abilities. The good news is that the brain—or organization—can be exercised and enhanced to produce the new skills and abilities.

The ideas, techniques, and exercises that follow in this book will provide new brain aerobics for you. They will increase your ability to develop new ideas, to be more responsive to new situations, and to feel confident in your ability to tap into the unlimited capability of your brain. In other words, they will help develop your intellectual capital.

ACTION SUMMARY

"People who do things make mistakes, but not the biggest mistake of all—doing nothing."

—Benjamin Franklin

- Take an inventory of your intellectual capital. How are you supporting it?

- What parts of your hard asset base have become insignificant to your success? Can you move ahead faster if you outsource some "hard asset" jobs?

- Hold a session with employees to ask how more of their brainpower could be better used. Consider programs like paying for employee suggestions.

- Set up training programs, or budget for outside training to foster ongoing learning and growth in your people.

Chapter 2

SHARING OF MENTAL MODELS
Prerequisite for Organizational Innovation

Edward and Monika Lumsdaine

Edward Lumsdaine, PhD, has been a management consultant at Ford Motor Company for the last two years. His wide interests during his tenure as a professor, followed by thirteen years as Dean of Engineering for three different universities expanded over time from heat transfer, fluid mechanics, aeroacoustics, solar energy, product quality, and continuing education using computers to how people learn and can become more creative. He has had assignments at Boeing, NASA-Langley, Cal Tech, Motorola, UNESCO, and many other organizations in the U.S. and abroad. He received the 1994 Chester Carlson Award from ASEE/Xerox for significant innovation in engineering education.

Monika Lumsdaine, a technical writer and award-winning solar home designer, has been team-teaching creative problem-solving classes and workshops for the last ten years with her husband Edward in industry, universities, and secondary schools. Since 1993, she has worked as a certified HBDI practitioner, management consultant for corporate behavior, and researcher into the thinking preferences of engineering students. She is president of her own company and a graduate of New Mexico State University with a BS degree in mathematics.

Edward Lumsdaine, PhD, Professor of Mechanical Engineering, Michigan Technological University, Houghton, MI 49931; phone (906) 487-2977, fax (906) 487-2822; e-mail lumsdain@mtu.edu.

Monika Lumsdaine, E&M Lumsdaine Solar Consultants, Inc., 1300 Cedar Street, Hancock, MI 49930; phone/fax (906) 482-0163; e-mail lumsdaine@arrownet.com.

Chapter 2

SHARING OF MENTAL MODELS
Prerequisite for Organizational Innovation

Edward and Monika Lumsdaine

"When organizations innovate, they do not simply process information—from the outside in—to solve existing problems or adapt to a changing environment. They actually create new knowledge and information—from the inside out—to redefine both problems and solutions and, in the process, to re-create their environment."

—I. Nonaka and H. Takeuchi, *The Knowledge-Creating Company*

How can your vision of creating a more innovative organization become reality? You might have tried training programs to increase creativity and innovation. But, for the most part, training efforts are ineffectual in producing permanent improvement in behavior and performance.

The reason for this failure is that training programs concentrate almost exclusively on transmitting *explicit* knowledge. Provisions for acquiring the crucial *tacit* knowledge are frequently lacking because the need is not understood. But innovation happens when explicit and tacit knowledge interact in a dynamic process.

This chapter will show how you can create and optimize the conditions for innovation.

EXPLICIT KNOWLEDGE: THREE MENTAL MODELS

Like the piers of a bridge, the three mental models—*thinking preferences, knowledge creation,* and *creative problem solving*—support all aspects of an organization's operation and output (see Figure 1). Figure 2 shows the "exploded" view of a bridge pier of Figure 1 and depicts how the three mental models build on each other. When organizations share and understand these mental models, the results are enhanced communication and teamwork, accelerated knowledge creation, improved learning and information management, and increased creativity and innovation. A case study illustrates how the models can be applied to improve a high-tech

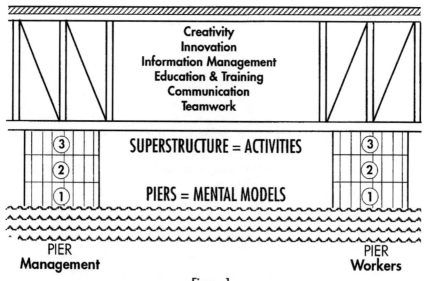

ROADWAY = OUTPUT
Competitive Products and Services

Creativity
Innovation
Information Management
Education & Training
Communication
Teamwork

SUPERSTRUCTURE = ACTIVITIES

PIERS = MENTAL MODELS

PIER
Management

PIER
Workers

Figure 1
Key Role of Mental Models to Support Organizational
Functioning and Innovation

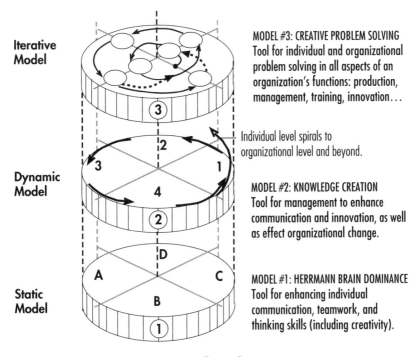

Iterative Model

MODEL #3: CREATIVE PROBLEM SOLVING
Tool for individual and organizational problem solving in all aspects of an organization's functions: production, management, training, innovation...

Individual level spirals to organizational level and beyond.

Dynamic Model

MODEL #2: KNOWLEDGE CREATION
Tool for management to enhance communication and innovation, as well as effect organizational change.

Static Model

MODEL #1: HERRMANN BRAIN DOMINANCE
Tool for enhancing individual communication, teamwork, and thinking skills (including creativity).

Figure 2
Relationship Between the Three Mental Models

education and training program. The models show how problems in the program can be traced back to a lack of understanding and appreciation of different thinking styles, omitted steps in the knowledge creation cycle, and a lack of training in creative problem solving.

Model #1
THINKING PREFERENCES:
THE HERRMANN BRAIN DOMINANCE MODEL

Each person thinks and behaves in preferred ways that are unique to that individual. These dominant thinking styles are the result of the native personality interacting with family, education, work, and social environments.

People's approaches to problem solving, creativity, and com-

municating with others are characterized by their thinking preferences. For example, one person may carefully analyze a situation
before making a rational, logical decision based on the available
data. Another may see the same situation in a broader context and
look at several alternatives. One person will use a very detailed,
cautious, step-by-step procedure. Another has a need to talk the
problem over with people and will solve the problem intuitively.

Ned Herrmann's years of research into the creativity of the
human brain led to the development of the Herrmann Brain
Dominance Instrument (HBDI). The instrument presents a graphical profile of an individual's preferences for, and use and avoidance
of, various thinking modes. The metaphorical model divides the
brain into left and right halves, and into the cerebral and limbic
hemispheres, resulting in four distinct quadrants (see Figure 3).
Recent research supports the validity of this model.

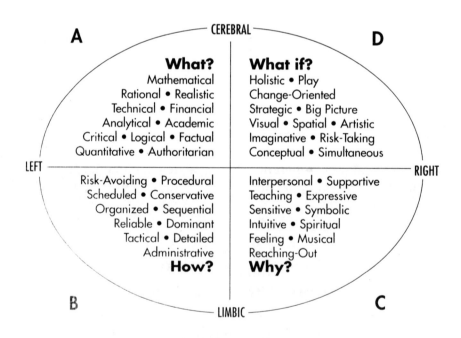

Figure 3
Thinking Characteristics and "Clues" of the
Four-Quadrant Herrmann Brain Dominance Model

All Thinking Modes Are Valid

The Herrmann profile results are value-neutral: there are no right or wrong answers. However, certain professions exhibit typical *average* profiles. For example, engineers and accountants tend to show a strong preference for analytical, quantitative, fact-based, quadrant A thinking, and tend to avoid the interpersonal, emotional, intuitive, quadrant C mode. Social occupations (counseling, nursing, teaching) have the opposite average profile with strongest preference in quadrant C and least preference in quadrant A.

The Four Thinking Quadrants Involved in the Planning and Design of a Bridge

Quadrant A
- Technical specifications
- Financing
- Practical project logistics

Quadrant D
- Future traffic projections
- Different possibilities
- Artistic design concepts

Quadrant B
- Low-risk, efficient path for getting from point x to point y
- How to build it

Quadrant C
- Connecting people
- Effect on communities and environment
- Politics

Beam Me Up, Scotty

The original Star Trek Enterprise is a good example of the four thinking styles depicted in Figure 3. Captain Kirk is an upper, right-side visionary. Spock is an upper, left-side second in command. Scotty is the lower, left-side detail man. McCoy is the lower, right-side understanding supporter.

—CSC Index Consultants

Multiple Preferences

Most people have at least two strong thinking preferences. Through motivation and practice, additional thinking preferences can be developed. When several thinking modes are habitually used by an individual, or purposefully available to a team, the likelihood increases that new ideas and concepts will be created and implemented.

A whole-brain team—representing strong preferences in all four quadrants—can produce optimum problem-solving results. But the team members must learn to understand each other and appreciate the contribution each person's strengths can make to the team. Thus, a common understanding of the Herrmann model is empowering. It is valuable for teambuilding, communication, training, management, knowledge creation, and innovation.

Model #2
THE KNOWLEDGE CREATION MODEL: A DYNAMIC PROCESS

The knowledge creation model we propose is based on concepts presented by I. Nonaka and H. Takeuchi in their book, *The Knowledge-Creating Company: How Japanese Companies Create the Dynamics of Innovation.* Their book presents a detailed theory

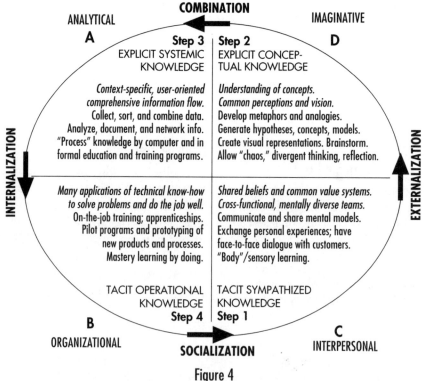

Figure 4
The Knowledge Creation Process Superimposed on the Herrmann Model

of the knowledge creation process as practiced in Japan.

As we read this fascinating work, we were struck by the correspondence between the knowledge creation model and the Herrmann model (see Figure 4). The Japanese model suggests four steps which correspond to the thought types of the Herrmann model:

Step 1: a collective commitment and "feel" for knowledge;

Step 2: intuitive understanding of concepts to ultimately result in organizational change, and increased innovation;

Step 3: synthesis of new knowledge through combination, and continuous improvement through feedback; and

Step 4: implementation and administration, plus extension to a higher organizational or external level triggered by the new experiences.

Model #3
THE CREATIVE PROBLEM SOLVING MODEL: AN APPLICATION AND INTEGRATION

From our research on creativity, and from an early brainstorming manual written for engineers, we developed a "whole-brain" problem-solving model to teach anyone to be more creative (*Creative Problem Solving: Thinking Skills for a Changing World*). The model integrates the right-brain thinking steps with the left-brain modes that are so heavily emphasized in our Western educational systems. Though we were unaware of the Herrmann and Knowledge Creation models at the time, in many ways, our model integrated the two.

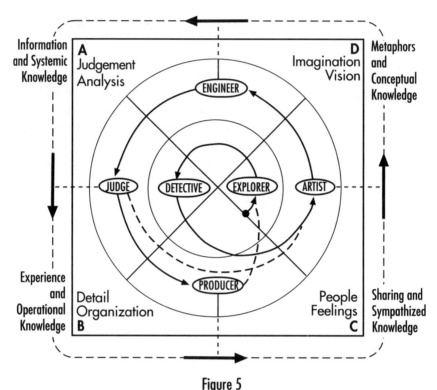

Figure 5
The Creative Problem Solving Model and Associated Metaphors Superimposed on
the Herrmann and Knowledge Creation Models

A Six-Step Cycle

The creative problem-solving process iteratively cycles through all four thinking and knowledge-creation quadrants (see Figure 5). Each stage in the process is associated with a corresponding metaphor or mindset. The *explorer* and *detective* stages discover and investigate the "real" problem and its context, and then define it in terms of a positive goal. The *artist* brainstorms many ideas. The *engineer* synthesizes the better ideas. The *judge* determines the best solution. And the *producer* puts it into action.

Hints for Managing the Knowledge Creation Process

The optimum management style for knowledge creation is neither top-down nor bottom-up. In this model, middle managers are not superfluous but form a crucial bridge in organizational functioning and continuous innovation.

Middle managers interact directly with two types of knowledge practitioners. *"Knowledge operators"* function in the area of tacit knowledge generation, whereas *"knowledge specialists"* deal primarily with explicit, structured and technical knowledge not necessarily of immediate interest to the operators.

Operators are salespeople interacting with customers. They are experienced production line workers, skilled craftspersons, or hands-on experimenters with in-depth local knowledge (for example, test drivers living in a particular country).

Specialists include R&D scientists, marketing researchers, design and software engineers, as well as finance, personnel, and legal staff. The knowledge creation process is enhanced when middle managers act as mediators to optimize the teamwork and communication skills of the practitioners and develop competencies in all four thinking quadrants.

Western organizations are strongly oriented toward explicit knowledge, especially analysis. The focus is on individuals. Japanese organizations are oriented toward tacit knowledge, with emphasis on experience. They focus on teams. Today's globally competitive world requires an understanding of both approaches for integration and cooperation in multinational enterprises.

Shine Up Your Creativity

To change your organizational culture from "killing" creativity to rewarding it:

- give your employees permission to be creative and take independent action
- encourage your employees to maintain a portfolio of creative accomplishments
- provide advanced creativity training for interested individuals
- provide basic workshops which present the three foundational models, with the expectation that employees use this knowledge to help achieve peak work performance

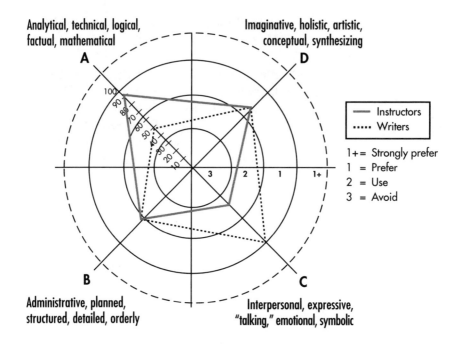

Figure 6
Average HBDI Profile of Instructors and Manual Writers

CASE STUDY: USING THE THREE MODELS TO IMPROVE A TRAINING PROGRAM

The three models can be applied to anything that could be improved with creativity and innovation. We are using the example of a training program to demonstrate the use of these foundational thinking tools to analyze problems and find solutions. Had these models been integrated into the development of the program right from the start, the current direction and outcomes would have been quite different and more innovative.

During the past two years, we have been involved in the development of a high-tech training program. Enormous challenges had to be faced and quickly resolved in an environment operating under severe time constraints. These included coordinating among the industry, government, and university partners; hiring, training, and certifying the "right" faculty; developing a curriculum; and building a training facility. The critical goal was for employees to quickly ramp up to high productivity.

Applications of the Herrmann Model (HBDI)

As shown in Figure 6, a mismatch was diagnosed between the thinking preferences of many of the instructors (mostly quadrant A) and the manual writers (mostly quadrant C). This has been difficult to resolve because of the strong communication barriers between the two groups, particularly when the people involved did not share this model to understand their differences.

Recommendations. With the organizational emphasis on teamwork, the HBDI should be widely implemented to foster an understanding of the importance of quadrant C and quadrant D thinking to the future success of the organization. This should involve many aspects of management, such as forming heterogeneous problem-solving teams and matching people's preferences and competencies to the job requirements. New staff people may have less respect for the power of the brain dominance model than frontline workers. An understanding of this model is crucial, since both knowledge creation and creative problem solving build on it.

Applications of the Knowledge Creation Model

We have only recently begun to use this new model to better understand why certain aspects of the training program worked and why changes were needed.

STEP 1—Socialization. The manager schedules frequent informal meetings (for sharing information and experiences) and celebrations of successes. These provide an opportunity for knowledge operators and knowledge specialists to meet and arrange further dialog for specific problem solving.

WORKING TOGETHER
"People have always had distinct preferences in their approaches to problem solving.... Today's pace of change demands that these individuals quickly develop the ability to work together. ...Rightly harnessed, the energy released by the intersection of different thought processes will propel innovation."

— D. Leonard, Professor, Harvard Business School, and S. Straus, organizational consultant

STEP 2—Externalization. One important management goal was to significantly shorten "ramp-up" time to full productivity—enabling the trainees to do their jobs with the new software as quickly as possible. Past experiences in many large companies have shown that on the average, ramp up to full productivity takes at least eight months, and many employees can take much longer. Thus a time reduction would yield substantial cost savings.

It was interesting to see how the ramp-up graph captured the imagination of management. It confirmed the importance of conceptualizing the vision in graphical or metaphorical form.

STEP 3—Combination. Surveys gave information and feedback on the training needs of different types of employees. This helped to streamline and custom design the curriculum as well as improve the manuals. A major organizational focus is on converting existing product information to "libraries" accessible with the new design tool. Once these standard parts and components are available, designers will be able to focus on combining them in more innovative ways. Overall, the bulk of the training is concentrated in this step of teaching explicit knowledge.

STEP 4—Internalization. When it became obvious that explicit knowledge acquisition in the classroom (even when supplemented with hands-on lab exercises) was not sufficient to enable trainees to do their jobs, on-the-job training became imperative. Instructors and student assistants were cycled to job sites to be available for at-elbow support and just-in-time learning (and to themselves learn the tacit knowledge required for

---

Gnosis Executives: The Knowledge Creators

"Gnosis" means Knowledge in Greek. The most important principle of business survival is the invention of knowledge. Gnosis executives push others to explore unknown territories. In this way, Gnosis executives expand knowledge, and build teamwork and consensus.

—Dr. Jack V. Matson, Leonhard Innovation Center for Enhancement of Engineering Education, Pennsylvania State University

applying the new software in product design and development). To improve the process even further, instructors are now being paired with application engineer mentors. A continuing problem is the lack of tacit knowledge about the company's products by the software designers. To overcome this problem, the developers are being paired with experienced product designers.

Expansion spirals. User groups are encouraged to share experiences to "spiral up" organizational knowledge, as well as extending it to supplier companies. The college instructors are planning to completely change the design courses when they return to their campuses—the explicit and tacit knowledge learned while in industry has changed the way they teach and has given them a conceptual understanding of the needs of industry. In essence, they have been prepared for introducing innovation in education.

Insight and Recommendations. The knowledge creation model reinforces the idea that the training program has to be a whole-brain process. To kindle excitement and imagination at the front lines, the program needs a "catchy" metaphor to link the organizational long-term leadership vision with the responsibilities and goals of the individual employees.

The feedback loop from the users was important and allowed rapid change in direction for continuous improvement in training. Having an organizational structure that was not cast in concrete was helpful. Experience showed that a cooperative project between industry, government,

---

Developing New Products

There are two different approaches to developing new products: You can be "for" the market or "of" the market. "For" firms depend on data collection, manipulation, analysis, marketing plans, and the latest MBA techniques to understand what the market wants. "Of" firms offer products to the market that they, personally, like. These firms are much more intuitive and nonanalytical. If their personal taste is in touch with the market, they can be quite successful, particularly in developing new lines of products that previously have not been available.

—Tom Peters

and universities can only work when all three have the freedom to be flexible and can react quickly to change.

Examples, team exercises, and application projects, as well as user hints, should be added as they become available to strengthen tacit knowledge acquisition. Had the knowledge creation model been available, attention could have been paid to strengthening the tacit knowledge acquisition right from the beginning, and the tremendous investment made in developing the traditional training classrooms might have been much smaller.

Knowledge creation is a new model which offers exciting possibilities for organizational design and management to achieve innovation. The case studies discussed in Nonaka and Takeuchi's book give a wealth of practical applications of the model which we cannot do in the limited scope of this chapter.

The Value of Knowledge

- Knowledge management should be part of the overall culture, not segregated as a separate function.
- Information systems have to be easy to use. Every employee has to be able to save and find information.
- Technological mechanisms to capture knowledge should be built around business problems and be human centered.
- Knowledge has to be moved quickly throughout the organization to improve innovation.

—Arthur Andersen and the American Productivity and Quality Center

---

Innovation for the Future
by Peter Drucker

From now on...innovation will have to be built into existing organizations....An established company that, in an age demanding innovation, is not capable of innovation is doomed to decline and extinction. And a management that...does not know how to manage innovation is incompetent and unequal to its task. Managing innovation will increasingly become a challenge to management, and a test of its competence.

The foundation of innovative strategy is planned and systematic culling of the old, the dying, the obsolete. Innovating organizations spend neither time nor resources on defending yesterday. Only systematic abandonment of yesterday can free the resources, and especially the scarcest resource of them all, capable people, for work on the new.

INTEGRATION WITH THE CREATIVE PROBLEM-SOLVING MODEL

In our example, the organization as a whole took a tremendous risk when top management made the commitment to adopt the new software and convert the entire global enterprise to its use over a four-year span. However, the problem of how to get people to change was not explicitly addressed. Training in creative problem solving would facilitate the switch to new paradigms and learning. In our changing world, what we know well—the way that was successful in the past—can hurt us if it keeps us from flexible, innovative thinking and trying "different" approaches.

Resistance to change and barriers to risk-taking with innovation at the front lines are pervasive. Integrating the three models into training can be crucial for success, because it can spread understanding to the entire organization. In the long-term, sharing mental models will ultimately lead to cost savings and true innovation. And, along the way, more people will be able to use their different mindsets productively, with greatly enhanced group harmony.

ACTION SUMMARY

"Putting good ideas into action is like giving birth-easy to conceive, hard to deliver, but well worth the labour."

—Ernest G. Tannis

Here are three Tacit Knowledge Exercises:

- In a small group, share examples of strong thinking preference "clues" as observed in behavior and communication. What insight have you gained into your own preferences? How might you enhance the mental diversity of your group?

- Apply the knowledge creation model to a project in your organization. Identify aspects of the project with each quadrant of the model. Which areas should receive more attention to strengthen knowledge creation and the innovation spiral?

- In a group of three, apply creative problem solving to a "small" problem. Try to cycle through all the mindsets in an hour or less. Use a flipchart or storyboard to capture sketches, the generated ideas, and the developing solutions, syntheses, optimizations, and implementation plans. What have you learned about the framework? Then analyze your experience using the knowledge creation model to discover parallels.

Action Checklist:

- Does your communication address all four thinking quadrants? You can assume that a work force of 50 or more people will have a balanced distribution of thinking preferences.

- Do the people in your organization understand the source of creativity and innovation—do they understand and appreciate their own thinking preferences and that of others?

- Are the three mental models integrated into the everyday functioning of your organization, as well as in all training programs (explicitly and tacitly)?

- To solve significant problems, are you using cross-functional, mentally balanced teams?

- Are you aligning your employees' thinking preferences with work assignments to increase productivity and "turn them on" to their work?

- Are you nurturing innovation "champions" and new paradigm "pioneers" to develop a strong support base for change and innovation?

PURPOSEFUL CREATIVITY
The 6 Ps of Creative Problem Solving

Jim Pierce

Jim Pierce has 17 years of experience making things work in the real world. He is a consultant with the St. Onge Company, an independent engineering firm focused on creative solutions and strategies in manufacturing, distribution, and logistics.

Mr. Pierce provides facilitation, training, and leadership in business strategy development, process reengineering, and creative problem solving. He facilitates workshops (public and private) focused on Purposeful Creativity in business problem solving and in the application of creativity to strategy development. He has a special interest in the practical application of systems thinking, breakthrough thinking, and lateral thinking in strategy development and organizational change. Some of his customers include: Tropicana, Pfizer, Procter & Gamble, and Ford Advanced Manufacturing.

Mr. Pierce has an MS degree in Industrial and Systems Engineering, and is a certified consultant in de Bono's "Six Thinking Hats." He is a director of the Innovation Network and a Founding Fellow of Innovation University. He believes that "work tomorrow will be vastly and fundamentally different from today, and the change will be led by people with new vision, tools, and skills."

Jim Pierce, St. Onge Company, 1407 Williams Road, York, PA 17402; phone (717) 840-8181 x3628; fax (717) 840-8182; e-mail JVPJR@aol.com.

Chapter 3

PURPOSEFUL CREATIVITY
The 6 Ps of Creative Problem Solving

Jim Pierce

"True creativeness is finding new possibilities in old situations."

—J.G. Saxe

Everywhere we look, we see the words "creative" and "innovative."

Flip through any magazine and you will see advertisements from companies ranging from hair salons to major global corporations trumpeting their creative products and services. Why are we attracted to the words "creative" and "innovative"? Because we're all looking for solutions to our problems—and the old answers often don't work anymore.

The rate of change—in the business world and society as a whole—is accelerating at an astounding pace. We're being bombarded by more and more changes, brought about by technological innovations, expanding global markets, and societal changes. Organizations, from the smallest to the largest, can adapt to these changes by applying creativity and innovation techniques to many business practices, including decision-making, idea generation, strategic planning, and problem solving.

THE 6 Ps

Purposeful Creativity is an innovation process that integrates the left side of the brain (the purposeful side) with the right side (the creative side). The process involves six components. The 6 Ps of Creative Problem Solving are:

- Problem
- Playing
- Perspective Future
- Percolate Ideas
- Participation
- Planning

PROBLEM

The focus of Purposeful Creativity is problem solving. Problems motivate us to consider new approaches, services, products, or relationships. Consider the following two problems.

MANUFACTURING GROWTH PROBLEM: A manufacturing company has had a 50 percent growth rate for the past five years due to a breakthrough product. The number of units manufactured and sold has more than doubled every two years.

PROBLEM: *What change is necessary to double production over the next two years?*

TURNOVER PROBLEM: A service organization is experiencing 50 percent employee turnover per year. The organization has 500 employees; every year they lose 250 and retrain 250 new people. This turnover not only impacts on operating costs, but on the quality of service and throughput (not to mention the emotional tension it creates in the remainder of the organization).

PROBLEM: *How might we reduce the turnover percentage from 50 percent to 1 percent?*

Visual Mapping

The ramifications of a change or problem are sometimes obvious, other times not so obvious. To quickly understand the scope and breadth of the problem (current reality), visual mapping is a beneficial technique. The group facilitator directs the problem solvers to consider the problem and individually list all areas of impact. The areas of impact are then posted on flipcharts and grouped by category. The team identifies how the different areas relate to each other. This provides a high-level, visual-system perspective on the problem. It is important that the facilitator ensure that the customer is considered in this model. This visualization describes the current reality of the group and organization.

Visual mapping creates a larger perspective of the problems at hand. In the example of the manufacturing company that needs to double production, an area of impact that might be identified is a large order backlog—a waiting time of four weeks from order to shipment. Another impact area could be the fact that orders often consist of multiple products in a variety of configurations and colors, so the finished product sits in the warehouse waiting to accommodate the shipment of a complete order.

Precise problem definition is vital. However, the intent of working with Purposeful Creativity is to spend more time creating solutions than thinking about the problem.

"Every original idea starts off goofy as hell, then you add to it, take some stuff away, refine it and it becomes a neat idea."

—Joe McKinney, CEO, Tyler Corp.

PLAYING

Playing is the process that leads one toward a willingness and enthusiasm to contribute, participate, and take a leadership role in changing the current reality. With Playing, the idea is to suspend your belief in the current reality, to challenge firmly held attitudes and beliefs.

Overcoming Blocks

Current reality is often a roadblock to generating possible solutions to the problem. "Ownership" is another major factor that creates a natural block to a person's willingness to play.

Ownership is derived from the act of participation in, or creation of, the current reality. Frequently, the people attempting to solve a problem have actively contributed to the current situation. Whether the problem is a good one (50 percent growth) or a negative one (50 percent turnover), the ownership factor influences the ability of people to look beyond the current reality.

Encouraging Play

An effective way to overcome unwillingness to play is to ask questions like:

- How would someone outside the organization see this problem?
- How would your customer view this?

Playing is the willingness to challenge current thinking, alter the environment, change the current reality. When the group steadfastly endorses the belief, "If we can make things wrong, we can make things right," the players are ready. Without the willingness to play, nothing else matters. (For more on the related topic of humor as a creativity-enhancing tool, see Chapter 4).

PERSPECTIVE FUTURE

Perspective Future is the mechanism used to define the target or destination. Focusing on the perspective of possible futures allows one to create an environment which encourages change, transferring the ownership issue of the current reality (past and present) to the ownership of the future.

"Begin with the end in mind."
—Stephen Covey, *7 Habits of Highly Effective People*

The key to Perspective Future is the ability to visualize and articulate what the future looks like. In the manufacturing example, the problem solvers would be asked to "walk down the assembly line" two years from now, and then answer questions like:

- What do you see?
- What do you hear?
- What has changed in the past two years?

Visualize Possibilities

Often the power of the current reality is so strong that these kinds of questions will result only in looks of puzzlement, and thoughts of "What is this joker talking about? The only thing I see is how we assemble our product."

Keep asking questions focused on the future. How will the competition react to the introduction of a particular product or service? How do customers order? What do customers want? Use examples from the world around you. Tell "make believe" and "what if" stories. Move from the "here and now" to the "happily ever after." Paint a picture of the perspective future with words.

In the manufacturing growth example, the Perspective Future might include: no order backlog, all customer orders produced simultaneously or grouped together, no finished goods inventory (we make it, we ship it), customer customization of the product, and reducing shipment time to one day.

The perspective future, and the problem-solving group's understanding of this future, need to be so clear and compelling that they pull the group through the roadblocks of current reality.

In his book, *Breakpoint and Beyond,* George Land develops the concept of Future Pull, stating, "The power of Future Pull replaces the anchor of the past." Gerald Nadler, in his book, *Breakthrough Thinking,* discusses his "Solution After Next Principle," saying, "The change or system you install now should be based on what the solution might be when you work on the problem the next time."

With the group focused on the Perspective Future, the question becomes "How do we get there from here?"

PERCOLATE IDEAS

A large number of idea-generation techniques has been developed in the past 40 years. For best results, the idea generation process should be fast-paced, without evaluation of individual ideas as they are developed. It is important to recognize that the more ideas or possible solutions that are generated, the better the chance of discovering a truly astounding or breakthrough innovation. (See also Chapter 5 on brainstorming.)

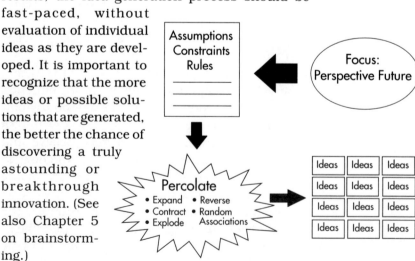

As a starting point, the group must focus on the problem and the perspective future solution. Each individual is directed to write ideas on sticky notes or $3'' \times 5''$ cards, using their preferred (normal) idea-generation methods (one idea per card). These ideas are posted and read aloud to the group, with no discussion or evaluation.

The next step is to identify which assumptions, rules, and constraints are being used by the group when considering the problem and perspective future.

> "A management that does not know how to manage innovation is incompetent and unequal to its task."
> —Peter Drucker

The known assumptions are important, but one must always search for those which are not discussed and not obvious. Imitate television's Lieutenant Colombo by asking questions that have no apparent relation to the problem being solved. Doing this will uncover rules and assumptions that are undercurrents and otherwise "unspoken." These unspoken rules, assumptions, and constraints are often historical ("We've always done that"), cultural ("We would never violate the distributor relationship"), political ("We can't consider doing away with that; it was the VP's idea"), or otherwise considered "untouchable."

In the manufacturing example, an unspoken rule may be that the current operations and procedures are the only acceptable ones, and that current production cannot be interrupted. In addition, there may be a strong belief that it is necessary to continue to satisfy customer demand during the transition to the "new solution." These constraints would likely generate solutions that would cause a doubling of space and a doubling of the current manufacturing process (and a doubling of problems).

Increasing the Idea Pool

Generate more ideas. Be daring. Change the rules. Explode them, contract them, reverse them, expand them. With this done, what do the possible solutions or ideas look like?

Another technique that provokes thinking outside of current reality is to have problem solvers consider the statement, "I am starting a new company and offering you the opportunity to join me if you can deliver the next breakthrough innovation." Or, "If you were the sole owner of this company, what would you do?" Fantasy-based questions often lead to reality-based possible solutions. Doug Hall (author of *Jump Start Your Brain*) suggests going through a dictionary and writing down every word related to your problem. The words stimulate many possibilities.

Another percolation technique uses random words and associations to generate additional ideas. Many creativity experts have their own versions of this technique, including Edward de Bono's Lateral Thinking, Doug Hall's Eureka Stimulus Response, and Arthur VanGundy's Product Improvement CheckList. In their books, each of those experts provides lists of words that can be used.

Other sources which provide word and picture associations can also be used, such as magazine advertisements, pictures, or dictionaries.

Visualize It

An excellent source of random words and visual stimuli is a children's product called

Sample Stimulus Words

Try to:	Make it:	Think of:	Take away or add:
bend it	adjustable	rain	handles
inject it	pocket size	genetic research	padding
divide it	self-destruct	disappearing ink	decorations
assemble it	grow	silent alarms	elastic

From Dr. Arthur VanGundy's Product Improvement Checklist (PICL).

Bear

Conductor

Tricycle

Microscope

StoryTime Cards. The StoryTime Cards are flash cards that have pictures and words such as Pirate, Parachute, Tricycle, Bear, Fire Truck, Secret Hiding Place. Using the random association technique can be difficult when working with adult business-oriented groups with diverse backgrounds, experiences, and beliefs.

The StoryTime Cards help overcome this diversity with a common ground (we all were children once), allowing the group to quickly create associations.

Each card illustrates a picture and the word that describes the picture.

The random word process begins by randomly selecting a card (or word) from the deck (or list).

Questions follow: "What is the concept of this picture/word?" or, "What association comes to mind with this card?" In our employee turnover example, for instance, if the word "tricycle" is randomly selected, an idea might be generated that describes a new organizational structure that has a powered wheel at its center which provides direction and pulls the rest of the organization along.

If the intent of the Purposeful Creativity effort is to build problem-solving skills of the group as you build solutions, consider a method to distinguish "normal thinking ideas" from those which are percolated, such as changing the color of the cards between each step of the process.

During the Percolation phase of Purposeful Creativity, it is best to generate ideas that are actionable, rather than conceptual. Concepts are easier to generate, but an actionable idea is more powerful and more adaptable to implementation.

PARTICIPATION

In group creative problem solving, Participation of all individuals is a fundamental requirement. It's often difficult for individuals with diverse experiences, knowledge, agendas, and levels of interest to create a collaborative environment.

There are many ways to overcome reluctant participation and personal agendas—including skillful facilitation and leadership—Edward de Bono's Six Thinking Hats® process has been specifically designed to generate a collaborative environment. The fundamental focus of this process is the transition from an adversarial approach to a collaborative approach, recognizing that different thinking modes are expected and required in transforming ideas to solutions.

In general, de Bono suggests problem solvers metaphorically wear different colored hats to represent particular ways of thinking. When everyone is instructed to wear a yellow hat, the group focuses on benefits; wearing black hats, the group focuses on risks or concerns; and so on.

de Bono's Six Thinking Hats®	
WHITE	based on rational information
RED	hunches and intuition
BLACK	risks and concerns
YELLOW	benefits and savings
GREEN	creativity
BLUE	controls the thinking process

The power of this type of methodology lies in the fact that all group members are considering the idea in the same thinking mode at the same time. Without a process that promotes collaboration, ideas are often tabled for consideration, immediately discounted, or tossed away because a "strong personality" intones, "That will never work, because...."

Collaborative processes keep ideas alive longer, allowing the opportunity for ideas to grow and blossom as they are discussed and developed.

PLANNING

Without planning, all you have is a party. You've played, generated ideas, and created possible solutions. Planning is the process of converting ideas to implemented solutions. What are the best ideas? How can these be selected from many?

An effective tool in the idea selection process is the "Potential/Ability" model. This process is effective because the group can quickly determine which ideas have the most potential.

Nine squares are drawn on a flip chart (or four squares can be used). The group considers the ideas that have been generated (and documented using sticky notes, cards, or paper). The ideas are evaluated based on the criteria shown in the figure to the left, or criteria selected more specifically by the group. The idea or possible solution is then posted in the appropriate square.

		Low	Medium	High
Perceived ability to implement	Easy	Easy /Low	Easy /Medium	Easy /High
	Medium	Medium /Low	Medium /Medium	Medium /High
	Hard	Hard /Low	Hard /Medium	Hard /High

Potential impact on business

For example, in solving the employee turnover issue, one idea might be to "establish a profile of employees who are likely to stay three or more years, and evaluate new employees using this profile." This may be considered Medium Ability to implement, and considered to have a High Potential impact on the business (Medium/High). The idea would be posted in the Medium/High block.

Ranking Ideas

Ideas that are considered Easy/High are the obvious first choice for expansion, further development, and implementation. The next two blocks

(Hard/High, Medium/High) require additional work. How do we transform this idea or possible solution from Hard/High to Medium/High or Easy/High? This is another opportunity to utilize idea percolation techniques.

The Potential/Ability model categorizes and focuses the group's attention on a select few ideas that need to be enhanced, fully developed, and possibly implemented. After the ideas have undergone this evaluation, more specific evaluation criteria may be applied to select the best to implement. For example, a company may have specific criteria for return on assets, return on investment, or schedule to implement.

Action plans should be utilized to convert ideas to implemented solutions. Visualization techniques which allow and require participation are effective for generating an implementation plan. Again, using sticky notes or 3″ × 5″ cards, the group lists specific actionable tasks and a target time for completion.

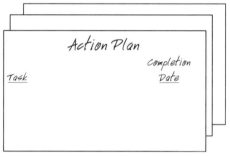

The more detailed and specific the identified tasks, the better the results. Optimum results are achieved by assigning the task to someone who will assume a "passionate leader" position versus a "designated task performer."

CONCLUSION

The term *Purposeful Creativity* was designed to embody appeals to both sides of the brain. The *Purposeful* activities appeal to the left brain, indicating a sense of order, a process, something that is logical and deliberate. The *Creativity* compo-

"Planning based on what's been done in the past is like driving a car when the windshield's painted black and you're navigating using the rearview mirror."
—Lindsay Collier,
Western New York
Futurists

nents ignite the right brain, producing a sense of invention, astonishment, and difference. (For more discussion of brain issues, see Chapter 1.)

This presentation would not be complete without emphasizing the importance of the Purposefully Creative Passionate Leader. In order to make new things happen, creative leaders must continuously stress focus, intensity, and a no-compromise attitude. Additionally, an articulation of the need for change must be continuously and consistently stressed and demonstrated.

When a Passionate Leader guides a group of problem solvers through Purposeful Creativity techniques, a transformation occurs. "This is how we've always done it, no win, hard work," becomes, "This is the Perspective Future; let's go there together." The Passionate Leader opens the doors to Purposeful Creativity. Purposeful Creativity opens the door to performance.

ACTION SUMMARY

"Action always beats fear."
—Bob Richards, Olympic champion

- First define your problem. Combine word and visual approaches by listing each aspect of the problem on a separate piece of paper and then arranging them on a flip chart by category.

- Second, suspend current reality. Play with the ideas involved, have fun, try different—even wacky—perspectives.

- Third, visualize and articulate what the future can be like. Play with different scenarios. See the end you desire and work back to the present.

- Fourth, percolate ideas. Generate many possibilities, then adapt them. Consider stimulus items like the dictionary, or children's picture sets.

- Fifth, involve everyone in a participative way. Use specific techniques like the Six Thinking Hats® to draw out people, collaborate, and control dominate personalities.

- Sixth, plan for implementation. Rate ideas on ease of implementation and their potential impact. Prioritize and move ahead. Purposeful Creativity requires integrity, a commitment to the process, and a viewpoint that recognizes that we can achieve the Perspective Future if we are purposefully creative.

Chapter 4

HUMOR AS A CREATIVITY TOOL
Laugh Your Way to Creativity

Randall Munson

Randall Munson
is the founder and president of
Creatively Speaking. He was
an IBM Program Manager at
the IBM Laboratory in Rochester, Minnesota. During his twenty years with IBM,
he led research and development projects with a variety of management,
programming, architecture, education, and marketing responsibilities. He holds
an MS in computer and information science from the University of Minnesota
and he is an adjunct professor at the University of Wisconsin.

In addition, Mr. Munson has been entertaining since 1972. He is a
professional magician, ventriloquist, and clown. He has received over 30 national
and international awards. His likeness has been placed on display in the Clown
Hall of Fame and the Smithsonian Institution. He is named in the *International Who's
Who of Professionals* and *Who's Who in Professional Speaking*, and has been
inducted into the Speaker Excellence Hall of Fame.

Mr. Munson is a rare combination of successful businessman and
sophisticated entertainer who educates and inspires organizations throughout
the world with his vital message about humor, creativity, and change. He has
delivered presentations to organizations including IBM, Disney, Norwest Banks,
US West, The White House, Burger King, and the Minnesota Vikings Club.

Randall Munson, Creatively Speaking, 508 Meadow Run Dr. SW, Rochester, MN
55902; phone (800) 294-1331; phone/fax (507) 286-1331.

Chapter 4

HUMOR AS A CREATIVITY TOOL
Laugh Your Way to Creativity

Randall Munson

"Men of humor are always in some degree men of genius."

—Samuel Taylor Coleridge

What were you doing at the time you got your last really creative idea?

Answer this question for yourself — right now.

That's right. Stop for a moment and think about it. Think back to a creative idea you came up with—you know, one of those "Aha!" flashes. The ones that make you pause and say to yourself, "Hey—I know—I could ..." Don't look for a revolutionary intergalactic breakthrough or the time you discovered the answer for world peace, just one of those times when a creative idea popped into your head.

Got it? OK. Now, what were you doing at the time? The question is quite simple yet it reveals a powerful truth about creativity.

I have posed this question to tens of thousands of people in audiences around the world. Here are some typical responses:

- "Taking a walk" (a marketing manager in Singapore).
- "While I was jogging" (a student in Boston).
- "When I was showering" (a corporate executive in Paris).
- "Driving my car" (a computer professional in Los Angeles).
- "Playing in the park" (an athlete in Australia).
- "When I was fishing" (an office worker in Minneapolis).

The backgrounds, experiences, and creative ideas of these people were extremely diverse, and the activities these people were engaged in when they got their ideas were varied. However, there is one amazing consistency. I have *never* had anyone tell me they get their great creative ideas when they sit at their desk and work really hard!

Working long hours, concentrating intensely, and pulling out your hair can inhibit creative ideas. If you want to come up with creative ideas, you need to try something else. The natural question is, "What should I try?"

HUMOR GENERATES CREATIVITY

Among the many techniques that prove to increase the flow of creative ideas, one of the most effective—and enjoyable—is humor. And, many other creativity-enhancing techniques, such as brainstorming, work best when approached in a playful, fun, humorous way. Yet humor is often overlooked as a technique.

In fact, humor and creativity are almost synonymous. A dictionary definition of humor is "the mental faculty of discovering, expressing, or appreciating ludicrous or absurdly incongruous elements in ideas, situations, happenings, or acts."

If you were to take the words "ludicrous or absurdly" out of the definition of humor, you would have a definition of creativity. One way to be creative is to associate elements not usually combined.

Humor in Brainstorming

Consider a brainstorming session. Brainstorming needs an open environment in which any idea can be freely expressed without fear of criticism. Successful brainstorming sessions are filled with laughter. After the laughter dies down, the participants often realize that the outrageously funny idea is actually a stimulus for a viable solution.

Try this. Immediately before starting to throw out ideas in a brainstorming session (with a group or with yourself) try a laughter opener. It can really help set the right mood for a wild, outrageous, and potentially productive session. Play a humorous recording to the group. Watch some Roadrunner or Pink Panther cartoons. Share jokes with one another. Watch a clip from a stand-up comic. Play some classic comedy like Abbott and Costello's "Who's on First." Share funny stuff from your own humor file.

Humor Overlooked As Creativity-Enhancer

In a survey of 24 creativity or innovation books, the majority (14) had no index listings for humor, fun, or laughter! Most of the 10 books listing at least one of these had no more than a passing mention.

"Wit consists in seeing the resemblance between things which differ, and the difference between things which are alike."

—Madame De Staël

DOWN GOES THE LAUGHTER, DOWN GOES THE CREATIVITY

I am going to share with you a logical rationale for why humor is effective in improving creativity so you can *understand* the reasoning. This is for you left-brain, logical thinkers.

I am also going to share some examples of humor so you can *feel* the value of humor. This is for you right-brain, experiential thinkers. Logically speaking, you should do the logical stuff first. So that is where we will start.

Laugh and Boost Your Creativity

Have you ever noticed how often little children smile and laugh? They spontaneously burst into smiles. Life, to them, is joyful and fun. A simple game of peek-a-boo can elicit uncontrol-

One study found that humor abounds in the families of creative children. There is almost constant joking, trick playing and family "fooling around."

—*Growing Up Creative,* Teresa Amabile

lable giggles. But try to play peek-a-boo with your boss and the response will probably be quite different! As we grow more, we laugh less. Pre-school children laugh or smile an average of 400 times a day. Adults, age 35 and older, laugh or smile an average of 15 times a day. Adults are losing 385 laughs a day!

"Life without laughing is sad." That statement is so profound you might want to write it down — I did.

There is something else that declines as we grow up. During the first five years of age, 90 percent of children are highly creative. However, during the next two years, ages six and seven, the percentage of those who are highly creative declines to only 10 percent. By age eight, only two percent are highly creative. The percentage of highly creative people over eight years of age remains stable at only two percent.

Creativity is generally defined as an unusual response. The fact is that young children are highly creative because they don't know how things are normally put together—so they come up with

"The secret of genius is to carry the spirit of the child into old age, which means never losing your enthusiasm."

—Aldous Huxley

many creative, wrong responses. As they learn, they get more "right" answers and become less creative.

LAUGH IT UP

Humor is a tool that allows you to be playfully "wrong" and look at ideas with fresh, childlike eyes.

"It's not by chance that I list having fun as my first suggestion on how to get your mind into idea-condition...in my experience, it might be the most important one."
—Jack Foster,
How to Get Ideas

A creativity test given to two randomly selected groups of people illustrated a relationship between laughter and creativity. The only significant difference between the groups was the activity they were engaged in immediately before taking the creativity test. One group listened to a serious, informative lecture on the subject of creativity. The other group watched movies. The movies were old black and white slapstick comedy films like the Keystone Cops, Laurel and Hardy, and Buster Keaton.

Though the two groups were demographically identical, the group that studied creativity before the test scored significantly *lower* than the group that had a good old belly laugh before the test. The people who had been laughing were more creative.

WHAT MAKES US LAUGH

"Humor in its first analysis is a perception of the incongruous."
—James Russell Lowell

When I perform as a stand-up comic or a professional clown and say something funny, audiences laugh. When I say something witty in a corporate board room, executives laugh. When I say the same kind of things at home, I often get no reaction. I once complained to my wife that when I'm at home with my family and do the funny things that crack up my public audiences, she and our children don't laugh. Her reply was quite insightful. She said, "Well, we expect that from you."

Here is a key to humor. Humor depends on the incongruous, the unexpected. If you already know the punch line to a joke, you won't laugh at it. Humor requires a collision of logic and absurdity. If you do what is expected, it isn't funny.

> "Man is the only creature endowed with the power of laughter."
>
> —Greville

Laughter Makes Us Creative

In the same way, if you do what is expected, it isn't creative. When you are involved in humorous situations—when you are involved in laughing—your mind is being whacked with surprises. You slide into the groove of seeing the unexpected. You delightfully anticipate the next twist. You become aware of different ways of looking at situations. You begin to see the world through different eyes.

When you see the world through different eyes, your perspective shifts. You discover possibilities previously unrecognized. You realize alternatives that had been concealed. You perceive new insights that are the key to further creative success. Creative juices are extracts from the lubrication of laughter.

When you see humor in a difficult situation, or problem, it is because you have looked at it in an unexpected way. When you see a problem from a different perspective, you are much more likely to see a new, creative solution. Humor results in fresh perspectives. In a problem-solving situation, when you can see the funny side, it helps you see a new solution.

Fun in the Workplace

Odetics, a robot maker, is "the wackiest place to work in the United States: The company encourages telephone-booth stuffing contests, bubble-gum blowing and similar activities to help employees have fun and unleash their creativity."

—*Industry Week* magazine

Listen and Laugh

People are better able to withstand stress and discomfort while listening to humorous recordings than while listening to relaxation tapes, informative narrative tapes, or nothing at all. Laughing can break open the confinement of stress and allow your creativity to emerge.

Stress: Creativity and Humor Killer

Stress is a significant inhibitor to creativity. When you are under stress and feel pressured, your thinking constricts. You tend to revert to your habitual thinking patterns. Fewer fresh ideas spring into your head. To be more creative, you need to pry yourself out of the bonds of stress.

WHAT IF THEY LAUGH AT ME?

Laughter can also be used as a club to kill creativity. Our instinctive reaction to ideas that don't conform to our expectations is to laugh at them.

Consider how many laughs were created by these once-outrageous ideas: Copernicus stated the earth revolves around the sun. Newton said there was some invisible force called gravity. Louis Pasteur claimed disease is caused by living creatures too small to see. Other well-known examples include Henry Ford who made a carriage without a horse. Orville and Wilbur Wright thought they could fly. John F. Kennedy said an American would walk on the moon within a decade.

Constructive Humor

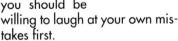

Humor can also be used to remind people of change. But you should be willing to laugh at your own mistakes first.

To change stodgy mindsets at Alagasco, a natural gas distributor facing lots of change and deregulation, the president uses a rubber stamp to imprint a dinosaur on any proposal that is too traditional.

—*1001 Ways to Energize Employees* by Bob Nelson

Over time each of these "funny" ideas have come to be accepted as significant and serious. William James captured the idea of this transition from laughter to acceptance when he said,

"First a new theory is attacked as absurd; then it is admitted to be true, but obvious and insignificant; finally it is seen to be so important that its adversaries claim they themselves discovered it."

If others laugh at your idea, don't assume the idea is bad. On the contrary, if they laugh at your idea, it may be a very good sign. The more unusual the idea, the greater the potential significance of its impact.

CREATE A PERSONAL HUMOR FILE

Your own humor file? Yes, your own humor file. If you don't have one yet, start it today. Whenever you run across something that makes you laugh, stick it in your file. It could be a cartoon, a quotation, a joke, an advertisement, a photo, a newspaper clipping—anything that makes you laugh.

By the way, you don't have to get anyone else's approval for the stuff in your humor file. If it makes *you* laugh, put it in *your* file. You are the only judge who counts.

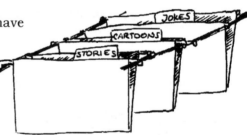

Samples from the Randall Munson Humor File

Here are some examples from my humor file. Remember, a humor file is personal, not because it contains personal information, but because it contains things that you, personally, find funny. My humor file contains the things that make me laugh. You may not find them funny. I hope you do though; that's why I'm sharing these with you. I'd love to make you laugh.

In the seat pocket on a Northwest Airlines flight, I found a placard describing the "Safety

Features" for the plane. You know, the instructions on how to evacuate the plane in case of a "water landing." (They actually use the term "water landing" on the PA announcement. Somehow I think bringing a 747 down on the ocean is more likely to be considered a crash than a landing. Maybe that is where we get the oxymoron "crash landing.") Anyway, on the front of the placard, in six languages, was the following statement:

> If you are seated at an exit and are unable to understand the information on this card, please contact a flight attendant.

That makes as little sense as the round sticker on the outside of a shrink-wrapped package of software I bought. The sticker read:

> Read carefully the IBM Program License Agreement located in this carton *before opening* this packet.

This reminds me of the instructions I found in the packaging of my new Lexmark laser printer. There were *three* items in the box that were labeled:

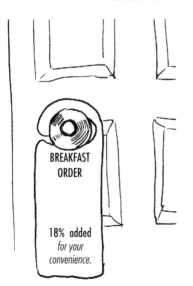

BREAKFAST
ORDER

18% added
for your
convenience.

Open Me First.

A Marriott hotel provided a tag for me to fill out the night before and hang on the door knob of my room to order breakfast delivered to my room. At the bottom of the tag was this statement:

> An 18% Gratuity will be added to your check *for your convenience.*

I called room service and told them they didn't need to go through all that extra work of adding 18% just for me. It would be just as convenient if they skipped the extra 18%. In fact, to make it really convenient, they could subtract 18% from my check. They didn't laugh.

I saw this sign on the luggage carts at the Newark Airport:

> Please Do Not Leave
> Child Unattended
> In Upper
> Compartment

Apparently if you want to leave your child unattended, you have to use the lower compartment!

At my seminars, I often show people copies of funny newspaper headlines or advertisements I have collected. I didn't include them in this book because some of them are copyrighted. However, I will share with you a statement printed in a newspaper that completely clarifies the copying question. It reads as follows:

> Do I need permission from the Pioneer Press to reprint an article or comic strip? Yes. Everything in the *Saint Paul Pioneer Press* is copyrighted and may not be reproduced without permission. Requests to reprint material from the Pioneer Press should be made in writing to (an address). *Please include a copy* of the article or the headline, author and date the article was published, and an explanation of how the material will be used.

Well, there you have it—samples from my own humor file. I hope you found them amusing. If not, that is all right. They are things that make me laugh. I use them when I need to counter my stress

Now Entering the Humor Zone

Eastman Kodak created a "Humor Room" with Woody Allen books, props, and comedy videos. People use it to take a break and stimulate their creativity.

Building a Curious Corporation

by Tom Peters

"What a distressing contrast there is between the radiant curiosity of the child and the feeble mentality of the average adult," Freud once wrote. Sad to say, he's got a point.

"Measure" wackiness. Consider having each employee submit a one-page essay on: the oddest thing I've done this year *off* the job, the craziest idea I've tried at work, or my most original screw-up, on the job or off. Using the answers to such questions, deal curiosity directly into the evaluation deck, near the top.

Model the way. If the chief isn't curious, then the troops aren't likely to be (and that's an understatement).

Teach curiosity. Brainstorming is not *the* answer to creativity. But it is *an* answer. There are techniques that can milk people's wackier ideas. Invest heavily in making them centerpieces of your firm's approach to solving *all* problems, mundane or grand.

Make it fun. Change the pace. Go to work next Thursday and declare it miniature-golf day. Hey, why not? Showing a training film this afternoon? Order popcorn for every participant. Curiosity has a lot to do with seeing the world through slightly cockeyed glasses.

or when I need the lubricant of laughter to get squeaks out of the pump for my creative juices. I encourage you to build your own humor file. It can help you break out of your thinking ruts— and besides, it is fun to find items for your file!

CONCLUSION:
HUMOR = CREATIVITY SNACKS

I hope you now understand more clearly that humor is a valuable natural resource that you can tap when you are looking for creative ideas. Remember, you had a great imagination as a child—back in the days when you laughed a lot. You can revive that natural creativity by remembering to laugh frequently.

We all can benefit from frequent creativity "snacks." Just as our bodies need food regularly to fuel our muscles, our minds need humor regularly to fuel our creativity.

Take a break once in a while (or even twice in a while) to nibble on a snack of smiles and laughs. Give your mind the fuel of fun to stoke the furnace of your creativity.

How long has it been since you had a truly great laugh? You know, one of those knee-slapping, side-grabbing, hiccup-

> "Probably the number one clue that creativity and transformation thinking are happening is laughter. Laughter and fun free the mind from barriers and restrictions."
>
> —*Transformation Thinking*, Joyce Wycoff

triggering, tear-generating, blow-milk-out-of-your-nose, and collapse-into-a-heap, kind of laughs. If it has been a long time, you may need more than a snicker snack. You may need a full seven-course funny feast.

Make the effort to have a meal of mirth. You may need to seek out a film, a comedy club, a cartoon book, a nutty friend, a good party, or a time of private silliness. Tickle your creative spirit.

There is a simple statement that summarizes everything I have been trying to say. I wish I knew who said it first so I could thank them. You may want to jot it down and stick it up where you'll see it often.

Laughter is the brush that sweeps away the cobwebs of your mind.

ACTION SUMMARY

"In creating, the hard thing's to begin."
—James Russell Lowell

- Make a list of the places or times you get your best ideas.

- Make a list of the things that make you laugh.

- Humor is in the eye of the beholder. Take a fresh look at the things around you for their humorous side.

- When things go badly, look for ways to laugh at yourself or the situation.

- Start a personal humor file today.

- Create a humor room or gather props in a box for those times when you need a quick humor "snack."

- When you need to be creative, refer to your humor file, or do things that make you feel playful.

Chapter 5

BRAINSTORMING

Rick Crandall

Rick Crandall, PhD, is a speaker, writer, and consultant, specializing in talks and workshops on creativity, marketing and sales, and change. He has spoken for *Inc.* magazine, the American Marketing Association, Autodesk, Office Depot, and the American Society for Training and Development. Dr. Crandall has presented well over 1,000 public seminars, given many keynote presentations, and worked with organizations from large law firms to the Air Force.

As founder and executive director of the Community Entrepreneurs Organization (since 1982), Dr. Crandall has run hundreds of brainstorming sessions.

He is the author of *Marketing Your Services: For People Who HATE to Sell* (1996), *1001 Ways to Market Your Services* (1997) and editor of *Thriving on Change in Organizations* (1997). In addition, he serves as editor and marketing columnist for *Executive Edge* (a national management newsletter).

Dr. Crandall is the recipient of an SBA Small Business Award, and is listed in various *Who's Who*s.

Rick Crandall, PhD; Agent: Select Press, PO Box 37, Corte Madera, CA 94976-0037; phone (415) 924-1612; fax (415) 924-7179; e-mail SelectPr@aol.com.

Chapter 5

BRAINSTORMING

Rick Crandall

"Men will always make mistakes as long as they are striving for something."
                                                            —Goethe

Brainstorming is the generation of ideas or possibilities. The secret to this process is for participants to be willing to make lots of "mistakes." The point of brainstorming is to generate a large *quantity* of ideas. Research shows that the more ideas you generate, the better your chances of coming up with a high-*quality* creative idea.

To do this, criticism and analysis must be suspended. Brainstorming was devised to encourage people to develop many ideas and "silly" ideas on the way to great ideas. Thus, in true brainstorming sessions, there is no analysis of the ideas and no selection of "final" solutions.

In this chapter, I'll discuss the key elements of brainstorming. Brainstorming can be a lot of fun—and it can produce great ideas!

WHAT BRAINSTORMING IS

Advertising legend Alex Osborn is credited with inventing brainstorming. In his 1948 book, he says that he began running regular sessions in his advertising agency in 1939. The rules he set out were:

(1) No "judicial judgment." No criticism of ideas during brainstorming.

(2) "Wildness" is welcomed. The crazier the ideas, the better.

(3) Go for lots of ideas. Quantity leads to quality.

(4) Combination and improvement of ideas are welcome.

I always start a session by stating these rules. I also tell participants that brainstorming does not involve discussion, except for brief positive comments like "Great!" The idea is to free associate quickly and briefly. Don't tell stories. If you disagree with a suggestion, don't say so, just make a different suggestion.

Laying out these ground rules before a brainstorming session is critical to its success. It is also helpful to explain to participants that making a decision involves three stages: generation of ideas, evaluation according to criteria, and choice. By acknowledging that brainstorming involves only the first step, you short-circuit distraction from people who want to analyze (that is, *criticize*) ideas.

The biggest problem in doing great brainstorming is that people won't "let go" and let

It Pays to Be Naive

Often the best ideas come from people outside the area being focused upon. This is because "outsiders" are unencumbered by the current "wisdom" in the field.

At one brainstorming session attended by a diverse group of people in business for themselves (including a landscaper, an accountant, a lawyer, and an inventor), a manufacturer presented a problem to the group. Many diverse ideas were generated. But the idea that ended up solving the manufacturing problem—and saving the manufacturer thousands of dollars—was generated by a woman who sold Amway products part-time.

themselves be uninhibited in their responses. To help participants be more free in their responses, remind them that since the "experts" on the topic have already thought of all the obvious ideas, what is needed now are crazy or naive suggestions that can later be changed or improved.

The Right Spirit

Osborn suggests that five to ten participants is the optimal size for a brainstorming group. The ideal group should include a variety of sophistication levels.

Only one issue should be brainstormed at each session. The topic should be as specific as possible and should be stated clearly at the beginning of the session. Osborn likes sessions that run about an hour. But sessions can be shorter—I've had success with sessions as short as ten minutes.

Osborn notes that the spirit of the session can influence the outcome. Perfectionist tendencies must be tossed aside. Sessions should be fun.

> "Humor breaks the self-censoring mechanism. It's hard to come up with ideas; it's harder to say them. But when we're laughing, we're less inhibited."
> —Jeffrey Mauzy, Synectics

Facilitation

At the start of the session, the moderator can throw out some silly ideas to stimulate others. I encourage people to talk out of turn if the energy is high. And when ideas are slow to come out, I'll call on people to overcome their holding back.

At less energetic sessions, there may be pauses between ideas with many people not participating. I've run hundreds of sessions for "untrained" groups where most people hesitate to speak. As a facilitator, it is important to reinforce people and prime the pump by repeating ideas or variations of ideas. Asking people what an idea makes them think of can start the flow of new ideas.

There are different approaches to moderating brainstorming sessions. Some moderators don't make any suggestions themselves. My approach

as moderator varies according to the group's behavior. If the group is generating ideas fast, I'll just
make encouraging noises and call on occasional
people who don't chime in. If idea
generation slows down, I'll make
suggestions that elaborate on
those already given, or call on
people for ideas. In addition, as
discussed later, I'll sometimes
provide new stimuli to which the
group can react.

Criticism inhibits the wild-
est and most creative ideas from
being voiced. Osborn emphasizes
that critics must be stopped.
Putting a halt to criticism is the
most important function of a session leader. (Ironically, even after very gentle comments to dis-
courage criticism, the critic often
takes offense at being criticized!)

If you have experts in the
group who "know everything,"
explain to them ahead of time
that if "wrong and dangerous"
ideas are expressed and seem to be accepted, they
still shouldn't straighten out the group. They can
make a note to share their wisdom after the
session !

How to Market

I facilitate a lot of brainstorming sessions where the topic is
how to market people's services.
The suggestions that come out
vary from the basics of marketing, "write an article for a trade
magazine," to the creative "as a
lawyer, work with a publicist and
a disaster consultant who might
refer people who have problems."

Brainstorming Without a Group

While counter to some definitions of brainstorming, brainstorming can be done alone. Without others' ideas to trigger your own, you lose some
creative stimuli. However, as I'll discuss later,
individuals brainstorming alone often produce
more ideas than brainstorming groups!

The "rules" for brainstorming alone are the
same as for a group—generate as many ideas as
possible, don't criticize yourself, etc.

WHAT BRAINSTORMING ISN'T

Many people who think they have been in a brainstorming session, haven't! A "bull session" is not a brainstorming session. A discussion group is not brainstorming. A community forum is not brainstorming. A focus group is not brainstorming. All of these formats may incorporate some aspect of brainstorming, but any technique or circumstance that allows criticism or discussion, or restricts the flow of ideas, is not brainstorming.

In any session without a facilitator, participants may have trouble sticking to the rules. Also, any session run by "the boss" will probably not be a good session. If people are trying to impress others or be politically correct, it can kill creativity.

Music to Brainstorm By

Play music at brainstorming sessions to set tempos and get brains in gear. Switch tempos— for example, from classical to rock—to wake people up and to stimulate participants to look at problems from a fresh point of view. Playing TV theme songs taps our collective psyche. Play the *Jeopardy* theme music to stimulate thinking, the *Gilligan's Island* theme to trigger playfulness.

—*Jump Start Your Brain* by Doug Hall with David Wecker

WHY BRAINSTORMING WORKS

Osborn had some opinions and research evidence about why brainstorming works. The main reason for brainstorming's success is the no-criticism rule. Too many people censure their own ideas before expressing them. Other factors that facilitate brainstorming include:

- *Contagion.* One idea stimulates another, both your own and others'.
- *Competition.* Some people will work harder to produce ideas when they are competing with others in the group.
- *Arousal.* It's possible that a good session can wake people up and literally arouse their creativity.
- *Fun.* The best sessions have humor and laughter as people throw out silly ideas.

Some environments encourage fun, others don't.

A reason for success that Osborn may have overlooked is the reward factor. The very act of setting up a group, and perhaps hiring an outside facilitator, lets participants know that creativity is valued. If ideas are considered valuable, there is more interest in the generation of ideas, even if there is no concrete reward.

A BRAINSTORMING EXAMPLE

It's hard to capture a live brainstorming session on paper. But it may be useful to you to see an example of the actual flow of ideas. The best sessions take on an energy of their own. Everybody enjoys themselves and feels free to speak out with their ideas, which come fast and furious.

Brainstorming Topic: How to Motivate Employees to Produce Ideas

To convey the spirit of brainstorming, I've taken suggestions from an actual brainstorming session and edited them into one stream. I won't try to show who said what, and I won't distinguish facilitator comments.

HOW TO MOTIVATE EMPLOYEES
TO PRODUCE MORE IDEAS

"Reward them for ideas."

"Use money or recognition."

"Pay them more."

"Dock their pay."

"Make it a game to produce ideas."

High-Class Pies

One woman came to the Community Entrepreneurs Organization for brainstorming. She had no business experience but liked to make pies. She had sold a few illegally in front of a gourmet market and didn't mind sales either. The group brainstormed and suggested that she emphasize the high-quality, handmade features. She then positioned her product as the high-quality, high-price pie. She now sells to hundreds of restaurants who appreciate the quality, as well as to supermarkets. She has built a million-dollar-plus business that is still growing.

Write First

Often, I'll have people in a group write down their first ideas for a few minutes before the group starts vocalizing their ideas. This gives participants ideas to keep the action moving, gets them in the habit of writing down their ideas, and gets some common responses out of the way.

"Make it a contest between employees or groups."

"Take a real game and look for ideas in it."

"Hold brainstorming sessions with them."

"Let them get silly."

"Don't let them sleep."

"Have a nap time story session where each employee tells silly stories to the others."

"Schedule a deadline for when ideas have to be produced."

"Create a method for people to exchange ideas."

"Have them talk with outsiders like customers and experts."

"Encourage drinking to loosen people up about ideas!"

"Hold a flame to the soles of their feet!"

"Provide them sex for ideas!"

"Confuse them."

"Put acid in their coffee" [presumably LSD!].

"Have nude encounter sessions."

"Meditation sessions."

"Hypnosis."

"Use art projects."

"Draw answers to questions on the wall."

"Play Pictionary."

"Have dancing and music."

"Screaming—with them or at them!"

"Plead with them."

"Threaten them."

"Create 'pop quizzes' on ideas to keep employees always ready with immediate ideas."

"Go to school—offer classes on creativity."

"Immediately hand out cash in front of everyone when a good idea is expressed, whether on schedule or unexpected."

"Paper the walls, etc. with sayings and ideas on creativity, plus good ideas of employees and who had them."

"Fire the most uncreative employee!"

"Create favoritism for those with the best or most ideas."

"Let employees vote on the best ideas and give away monthly prizes with a grand prize each year."

"Bring employees' children in for fresh views."

"Hold their children hostage until they produce great ideas."

Summary

A typical session would have lasted longer than the above extract did and, thus, would have produced many more ideas. But even so, you can see that the ideas range from the simple to the creative to the stupid. There are several themes and variations of themes. Some ideas follow directly from prior ideas. Some ideas are redundant. Some double back.

In general, early ideas tend to be less creative, unless you hit a wacky streak where unusual ideas feed off each other.

At DuPont, brainstorming is often used to start off a day of creativity. Often these first ideas that people bring with them are fairly commonplace. But by acknowledging them, you clear the way for more creative ideas. A good session can also be fun and loosen people up for more complicated exercises.

How Ideas Build on Each Other

In the book, *The Creative Problem Solver's Toolbox,* Richard Fobes repeats the idea generation path of a group of five people charged with inventing a vapor-proof closure for space suits.

One group member suggested using an insect to pull a thread through holes in each side of the closure—not a very practical idea, and one that could easily be laughed off and dismissed. But it prompted another team member to replace the insect with a steel wire coiled in the shape of a spring. While this idea, too, was impractical, it inspired yet another member to propose using two enmeshed springs, which eventually became the basis for the new closure.

ACADEMIC RESEARCH

When Osborn and others first started using brainstorming, they were guided by their common sense. Since then, hundreds of academic studies have accumulated. Most are not particularly creative! Many are little more than demonstrations of the basic technique. However, a few provide new information.

Groups Are Worse Than Individuals!

One of the basic assumptions about brainstorming by Osborn and others was wrong: Groups do not produce more and better ideas than individuals working alone.

In a brainstorming session with 10 people that lasts an hour, only one person can talk at a time. For a possible hour's worth of suggestions, 10 person-hours are invested. When the same ten people brainstorm alone, you have a possible 10 person-hours of suggestions.

Production blocking means that not everyone can talk when they have an idea to share. Some contributions are blocked while other people talk. Additionally, many ideas come and go through short-term memory. If you don't spit them out within a few seconds of getting the idea, they are gone. That's why I advise people in my groups to write down their ideas if they can't share them immediately.

In practice, the difference in productivity between individuals and groups isn't anything like

---

The Extended Benefits of Brainstorming

Most studies of brainstorming measure brainstorming effectiveness by the efficiency of idea generation. But the benefits of brainstorming are more far-reaching. A two-year Stanford University study of a product design firm found that brainstorming:

(1) supported the organizational memory of past solutions
(2) provided skill variety for designers
(3) supported an attitude of wisdom
(4) impressed clients
(5) provided income for the firm

10 to 1. When brainstorming solo, each individual isn't thinking of ideas for the whole hour. Also, when 10 people work alone, they produce a lot of redundant ideas. Members in brainstorming groups do stimulate each other. In groups, not all of the time is wasted when others are talking—people use the time when others are talking to think. But without specific techniques to intervene, groups will generate only about one-half to two-thirds as many ideas as the same people working alone.

HOW TO IMPROVE BRAINSTORMING

Fortunately, there are factors that can make groups as productive as individuals and improve brainstorming in general. So far three have been demonstrated:

- idea quotas
- better trained facilitators
- using computers

Idea Quotas

If you measure how many ideas one person produces in a given amount of time, you have a quota. By telling individuals or groups what good performance looks like in terms of number of suggestions, they produce more. A group given a quota can match the performance per hour of individuals who are not given quotas.

Better Trained Facilitators

One study compared trained student facilitators against groups with untrained facilitators. Unfortunately, the groups

Create a Product Line

An inventor wanted brainstorming on how to be more successful with his products. He had an "all-in-one" plastic ruler with 12 different scales. The group eventually suggested breaking it up into multiple products, with each scale available in different sizes. He tried it and his average order more than doubled as retailers tried a few of several new products, instead of a few of the all-in-one.

with trained leaders didn't perform any better! Then they gave the "trained" facilitators additional training. Groups led by these "super-trained" facilitators produced at the same level as individuals (on an ideas-per-hour/per-person basis). The good news is that group performance also increased over time.

Response Hierarchies. Brainstorming is really a form of free association. When we are given a problem (or stimulus), we have certain reactions. Our first reactions tend to the most common for our cultures, and thus not creative. It takes time and work to go "down the response hierarchy" to come up with more obscure or creative responses.

For instance, if people are asked to say the first things that comes to mind, in response to the word "dog," most people will say "cat," name a breed of dog, or give the name of a dog—Lassie, Rin Tin Tin, Spot, Fido and other names will come out depending on one's age and experience.

Few people would say "frog" as an early association to dog. However, it is quite direct in a chain of associations. (Budweiser beer used a dog named Spuds MacKenzie in ads for years. Today, they are using frogs and even talking lizards.)

Talking about response hierarchies that vary from dominant, common responses to "deep," rare responses is a technical way of explaining why well facilitated groups could increase their advantage over time. In the first period of brainstorming, almost everyone produces common associations. But after those run out, a well run group will continue to produce, or even increase, their production, thus generating more creative ideas.

Computer-Aided Brainstorming

One practical reason why a group can't produce as many ideas as the same people working individually is that group members can't all talk at once. A networked computer program solves that problem. These systems are currently rather expensive, but they can do some great things.

Using a computer system, everyone can type his or her responses in at the same time. Each person's responses can be anonymous. All or some responses can be displayed on a screen for everyone to see and react to. There are other related capabilities. For instance, in a postbrainstorming stage, choices can be ranked and voted on anonymously. Computer brainstorming can also be done with people at different locations linked together.

The only drawback to this method is speed—or rather, lack of speed. We can talk at 100 to 300 words a minute. Since few people can type even 50 words per minute, theoretically not as many ideas can get on the table in a computer session. However, in practice, few of us could talk without breaks anyway.

ADVANCED BRAINSTORMING TECHNIQUES

One advanced brainstorming technique has already been discussed—the use of computers. Many other individual creativity techniques can be used with brainstorming. For instance in Chapter 3, Jim Pierce mentions lists of words to stimulate new ideas. In a brainstorming session, the facilitator can throw out words, ideas, or concepts for people to relate to the question at

The SCAMMPERR Method

Alex Osborn identified nine main ways to manipulate a topic. Bob Eberle arranged them into the mnemonic SCAMMPERR. Michael Michalko developed a card pack (*ThinkPak*) with five cards for each of the nine "manipulations." For instance, for "Substitute" you can try substituting emotions, someone else's perspective, another material, another process, places, things, and so forth.

Substitute something
Combine it with something
Adapt something to it
Magnify or add to it
Modify it
Put it to some other uses
Eliminate something
Rearrange it
Reverse it

hand. For almost any problem, you could ask questions such as: "How could this relate to children?" "How does this relate to the color red?"

Written Brainstorming

An older variation of brainstorming has some of the properties of computer-aided brainstorming. With written brainstorming, participants write their responses on a piece of paper. Then each list is circulated to the other group members so they can add to it. With this method, you have both uninterrupted production by each person, and the stimulation of other people's ideas.

This technique can also be applied when people are physically separated. You can mail, fax, or e-mail a list of ideas to the next person (or multiple people). They can add to it and pass it on along your routing list.

Reversing a Problem

In one case, a group was out of ideas for improving customer service. After they had run down, I asked how they could *ruin* service the fastest. They laughed and easily came up with two dozen ways, some of which suggested new concerns of customers, and led to fresh improvement ideas.

Changing Problems

When the group runs out of ideas or energy on the stated problem, the facilitator can change the problem. A common approach is to suggest the opposite. For instance, using our earlier problem of how to encourage employees to be more creative, the problem could be turned around to ask how to make employees *less* creative. This will often produce a new group of ideas, many of which can be reversed and applied to the problem.

A similar approach is to ask the group to produce the worst possible ideas for a problem. For instance, for a bad way of putting out fires, you might come up with throwing a pail of gasoline on it. This could lead you to a fresh approach. (In fact, one way to put out big fires, such as oil well fires, is to blow them up.)

Forced Relationships

By forcing people to consider the problem against a set of other stimuli not usually associated with it, you create new ideas and possibilities. The SCAMMPERR technique essentially does this.

One common creativity test asks people to name as many uses as possible for a common object, such as a brick.

The first responses usually have to do with a brick's weight and hardness—for instance, use it as a weapon, to break windows, to crack nuts, and as a door stop. To improve creativity, force relationships by asking people how the brick could be used during sex, in aviation, etc. (It's a bad pillow for sex; a bad glider for aviation. But it's a good conversation starter for sex when painted by a famous erotic artist, and a possible parachute test weight in aviation.) The possibilities are endless, which means the creativity is too!

Mindmapping

Mindmapping involves putting ideas on a chart and trying to show relationships between them as they are generated. This provides organization and can stimulate new ideas. Many people don't consider this brainstorming. But someone has to record ideas during "regular" brainstorming. Why not write them on a chart and try to organize them at the same time?

Brainstorming as usually done is a highly verbal technique. That means people who aren't particularly verbal may not like it or contribute as much. As mentioned in Chapter 6, you can do

Sticky-Note Brainstorming

One consultant puts each idea on a Post-It® Note in a mind-mapping session. This means that they can be moved around as new themes emerge. In one case, only when two ideas were accidently side by side in the "don't know where to put it section" did the group think of a new relationship between the ideas that transformed their business approach.

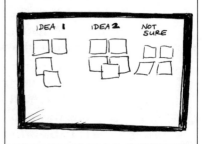

visual brainstorms. Participants can draw pictures, sort pictures, combine pictures, or whatever.

CONCLUSION

Brainstorming is a great technique. But it's not perfect. It can be seen as silly. People can resent being told to stop criticizing. And there can be a fear of failure.

On the other hand, brainstorming is usually a lot of fun. In a well-run session, participants feel involved in the ultimate solution. It helps group involvement and support—and, it's a nice break in the day's routine.

> ### How Sad!
>
> "Senior managers often say that creativity is all right for research or advertising or marketing but not for them."
>
> —Edward de Bono

Why Isn't There More Brainstorming?

Beats me! People are reluctant?

Many people misunderstand what brainstorming is. And very few people have been in a real session. There is some lack of skill in using the technique. But the really unfortunate thing is that most people and organizations feel that they are just "too busy" to be creative. They have no real goals for creativity and innovation. They're just putting out fires and "marking time."

ACTION SUMMARY

"The secret of getting ahead is getting started."
—Mark Twain

- To see the value of brainstorming, use it alone to generate new ideas. Focus on crazy ideas first. Then, at a later session, change them into practical ones.

- Look for problems that need new ideas and convene a brainstorming group.

- Set up a brainstorming bulletin board to collect ideas for solving a problem.

- Try pictorial brainstorming on a board or in a group.

- Give yourself or your group an idea quota. In one study, individuals produced about 120 ideas in twenty minutes.

- When you need ideas, try circulating a written brainstorming list of ideas around your organization or to your friends.

- See who's available in your organization to moderate sessions, or try it yourself.

- To avoid losing ideas in short-term memory, always jot down the idea when you can't say it immediately.

- When you run out of ideas, try to generate ideas to solve the reverse problem, or a different problem. Then adapt the new ideas to your issue.

Chapter 6

USING VISUAL IMAGERY TO ENHANCE CREATIVITY

Dorothy A. Sisk

Dorothy A. Sisk,
PhD, holds an endowed chair in education at Lamar University. Throughout her career, she has been intensely involved with the education of gifted and talented children.

Dr. Sisk is an international consultant focusing on leadership, communication, and creativity development. She currently directs the Center for Creativity, Innovation and Leadership at Lamar University. She received the Distinguished Leader Award from the Creative Education Foundation (CEF) in 1989, The Distinguished Service Award from the National Association for Gifted Children in 1983 and 1994, and the Creative Lifetime Award from CEF in 1994.

Dr. Sisk specializes in the field of creative behavior, leadership development, and multicultural training. She has conducted numerous training sessions throughout the U.S. and internationally. Some of her clients include Xerox, Turner Broadcasting Company, Procter and Gamble, Warner-Davis Park Lambert, American Cyanamid, AT&T, and Bell Laboratory.

Dr. Sisk is the author of numerous books including *Creative Teaching of the Gifted*, and co-author of *Leadership: Making Things Happen, Intuition: An Inner Way of Knowing*, and *Leadership: A Special Type of Giftedness.*

Dorothy A. Sisk, PhD, Center for Creativity, Innovation, and Leadership, Lamar University, PO Box 10034, Beaumont, TX 77710; phone (409) 880-8046; fax (409) 880-8384; e-mail SISK,D.A.@.hal.lamar.edu.

Chapter 6

USING VISUAL IMAGERY TO ENHANCE CREATIVITY

Dorothy A. Sisk

"You see things; and you say 'Why?' But I dream things that never were; and I say 'Why not?'"
—George Bernard Shaw

Visual imagery, or "seeing with the mind's eye," is often described as the language of the unconscious. It allows you to access the nonverbal parts of your brain. Numerous writers—from Carl Jung on—further suggest that visual imagery can expand creative thinking and problem solving, as well as develop self-awareness. For instance, a 1997 study found that high school students with high imaging abilities were significantly more creative.

When used as a creativity and innovation tool, visual imagery helps individuals view the workplace more clearly from different perspectives. When you visualize, you can use more of your brain, bring forward more creative possibilities, think in more concrete terms, and help set aside personal biases and assumptions.

In this chapter, several examples will show how visual imagery can be used to boost creativity. Potential pitfalls and problems will also be shared, as well as resources to assist individuals and trainers in using the techniques.

A HISTORY OF VISUAL IMAGERY

Visual imagery has a rich tradition dating back to ancient peoples who made little distinction between sleeping and waking states, and between visions and perceptions.

As early as 200 BC, writers reported the purposeful use of visual imagery. "Patanjali" describes three states of visual imagery:

- dharana, in which you simply focus on a given place or object;
- dhyana, in which you strengthen the focus of attention by using supportive gestures, such as hand movements or body postures; and
- samadhi, in which you experience a union or fusion with the object and cannot distinguish self from object; you feel a sense of being absorbed into the object.

Jung, in *Memories, Dreams, Reflections*, describes the imagery process, particularly samadhi, as a search for unity in mind, body, and spirit. To achieve the state of dharana, many Eastern cultures use mandalas (geometric designs symbolic of the universe used to help individuals focus).

An example of someone who used visual imagery with great success is Nikola Tesla. Tesla invented the alternating current dynamo and power transmission system that made the electric age possible. Tesla deliberately cultivated his ability to visualize.

Tesla reported that at seventeen he found that he was easily able to visualize inventions. He could construct, modify, and even operate his hypothetical devices by visualizing them.

When he could not get a clear image of what he needed, it would often appear later in his mind as a full-blown picture. For instance, once, when walking on the beach with a friend and discussing other things, a picture of a dynamo came to him like a flash of lightning. He drew the diagrams in the sand and later described the incident as a mental state of happiness.

Many famous inventors such as Edison have reported using dreams, or the state between waking and sleep to visualize solutions to problems they set themselves. One of the best known cases is August Kekule who worked on the structure of the benzene molecule for years. He dreamed of a snake biting its own tail and realized that a ring-like structure was the solution he'd been seeking.

> "Employing creative people is necessary in today's competitive world, but absolutely not sufficient...they need tools to help them to keep renewing creativity. That is what creativity techniques do."
> —Sheldon Buckler, vice-chairman, Polaroid

ROLE-PLAYING AND TAKING DIFFERENT PERSPECTIVES

The skill of visualization is far more than just the brain's ability to construct images or handle spatial relationships. Visualization also involves mental role-playing.

Visual imagery is a specialized form of role-playing and perspective taking. Many creativity exercises involve some form of role-playing. For instance, one problem-solving strategy is to look at a problem from different perspectives. A more specific technique is to imagine how famous people like Thomas Edison or Florence Nightingale or Leonardo da Vinci would solve the problem. Usually this also involves visualization. It's an easy technique for an individual to use, and can also be used in a group setting.

A group can discuss a problem with all participants taking on the same role. Alternatively, cards with the name of a personality can be passed out to the group and each participant takes on a separate identity. So you might have Santa Claus, Eleanor Roosevelt, Joe Montana, Bill Clinton, and Barbara Walters discussing potential new markets for a product. One creativity trainer at Kodak has a collection of hats that participants don to facilitate this role-playing process.

A last benefit of visualization, imagery, or mental perspective taking is that you can experiment and take risks in complete security. You can picture yourself jumping off a cliff and you'll remain perfectly safe. However, if you're good at visualization, you'll feel an adrenaline rush when you "jump!"

Visual Imagery Is Even More

Mental rehearsal is one form of mental role-playing and visualization that is frequently used in sports.

An early research study in this area divided basketball players into three groups. The first group practiced shooting free throws for a month. The second spent the same amount of time imagining themselves shooting free throws. The third—the control group—did neither. At the end of the study, the groups who actually shot free throws and imagined shooting them improved equally. As might be expected, the control group, who did nothing, did not improve.

The effectiveness of mental rehearsal can be explained by several factors:

- Your brain makes little distinction between vivid imagery and real behavior.
- Your brain neurons may fire to

"Imagery gives managers a fundamental edge in gaining access to intuition, creativity, and more complete assessments of business-related and interpersonal settings."
—Robert H. Bennett III, Walter J. Wheatley, Nick E. Maddox, and William P. Anthony, *Management Decisions*

strengthen connections in the same way, whether you're thinking of doing something or actually doing it.

- Mental rehearsal can be better than actual practice because you can see yourself performing ideally without the distraction of actual performance inconsistencies.

Many world-class athletes have used mental rehearsal to improve their performances. One of the best known is Mary Lou Retton who reported visualizing her gold-medal gymnastics routine the night before she won. It has also been used by many other groups (for example, NASA astronauts).

Mental Rehearsal in the Workplace

Mental rehearsal can be used to enhance creativity in the business world. Say you have to present a proposal to a finicky client. You can visualize the entire process: walking into the room, greeting everyone, looking at everyone sitting at the table, making your presentation, fielding questions, etc. By practicing various scenarios through your visualization, you gain confidence to be creative, the situation becomes less ambiguous, and you are less likely to be surprised by responses you hadn't anticipated.

Benefits to the Learner

Whether or not you're ready to replace your practice time with mental rehearsal, you'll find visual imagery a useful tool in many ways.

Visual imagery can be easily used by individuals alone, but it also has a number of strengths in group settings. Visual imagery motivates participants to personalize and react to learning. The group leader can use imagery exercises to call upon the inner resources of each individual learner. In this way, the exercises empower learners, have an immediate impact on their present situations, encourage self-knowledge, and demonstrate respect and appreciation for their inner lives.

Exercises in visual imagery

are consistent with principles of adult learning because they:

- encourage spontaneity
- respect choice
- call upon previous experience
- give opportunities for direct participation

SIX STEPS FOR TRAINING VISUAL IMAGERY

Following are six steps to support creative visualization. The first three steps are used to introduce a group to visual imagery. The last three steps can be used by either groups or individuals.

Step One: Warm-Up

Create a sense of belonging, trust, and mutual interest within the group. One way to build a sense of belonging is to ask the participants to introduce themselves, to share their understanding of visual imagery, and how they use it. As they relate examples from their professional and personal lives, they will expand their individual understanding of the technique and its merits. This warm-up time reaffirms the uses of the technique and highlights similarities and differences in the participants' responses.

Step Two: Background on Visual Imagery

Next, present a brief history of the technique, a simple working definition, and specific applications of visual imagery. This discussion will help familiarize the participants with the technique and provide an opportunity for them to ask questions. If individuals have concerns or fears, they can identify and discuss them at this time.

"The ability to visualize in detail is a key to success."
—Denis Waitley,
The Psychology of Winning

Step Three: Agenda

Share the agenda, including goals and objectives of the visual imagery session. The goals might be to:

- build individual skills in using visualization
- involve both "sides" of the brain
- increase the ability to use visual imagery creatively

Listing the goals establishes a sense of orderly learning and shows respect for the integrity of the participants. In the body of the workshop, participants may explore their understanding of themselves and others through specific activities. When participants fully experience an activity and process it by applying the insights to themselves, they will be more likely to use visual imagery effectively to become creative problem-solvers. This type of active learning, compared to more didactic learning, involves the intellect as well as the senses and enhances personal benefits from the technique.

Benefits of Visualization

"When we visualize, we are able to think in more concrete terms, overcome many personal assumptions, evoke much greater memory, and assess possible ramifications more creatively and thoroughly. The result is often a much larger and more detailed set of information on which to base decisions and forecast future scenarios."

—Robert H. Bennett III, Walter J. Wheatley, Nick E. Maddox, and William P. Anthony, *Management Decisions*

Step Four: Relaxation

Many of my ideas for using visual imagery as a creativity training tool derive from Gestalt psychology in which images, ideas, and connections create a whole—a gestalt. Several activities popularized by Gestalt psychologist Fritz Perls call for the use of a short relaxation exercise to increase receptivity to visual imagery.

For a group, use a modulated voice tone to slow the training process down sufficiently to provide time for participants to create images. These images eventually contribute to the gestalt. For example, you can say:

> Think of a place where you can be quiet. This can be a real place or a place that exists only in your imagination. Sit or lie down, whichever is more comfortable or preferable to you. Now, close your eyes and become aware of your breathing. Take several deep breaths, and count slowly to yourself, 1 to 7 on each inhale and 1 to 7 on each exhale.—Inhale 1, Exhale 1. Inhale 2, Exhale 2... (continue to... Inhale 7, Exhale 7).

The next exercise is to relax the entire body. Individuals can do this on their own. First instruct participants to tense their toes, hold them that way, then relax. Then have them tense their ankles, hold them, and relax.

Continue this exercise by asking participants to tense, hold, and relax their knees, thighs, hips, buttocks, stomach, chest, shoulders, arms, hands, fingers, necks, head, and face.

Following this process, ask participants to notice changes in each part of their bodies as they concentrate on them. Relaxation exercises will help participants experience visual imagery; however, an experienced "imager" can become quiet quickly and may want to use a mandala such as the one to the right to focus awareness.

Focusing on a mandala encourages the spatially oriented functions of the cerebral right hemisphere. I suggest that participants focus on the center of the mandala and become aware of their bodies relaxing. When you concentrate or focus on a visual pattern for five minutes or more, your inner dialogue is gradually replaced by a quieting process that encourages visual imagery. When you are relaxed, you are ready to proceed with guided imagery exercises.

Step Five: Self-Understanding Activity

The following activity is adapted from Fritz Perls's "Revisiting the House of a Friend." This activity uses imagery to build understanding of oneself and others. Give these directions:

Think of a house that you would like to revisit. Choose a memory that is not too distant or difficult for you to recall.

Now, close your eyes, and be aware of what you see. What do you see?

Is someone opening the door?

Are there other people?

Try to accept the images as they appear without conscious editing.

Allow yourself to go back to this remembered place.

Notice what is there, and hold on to the pictures.

As the pictures reveal themselves, you may find words linked to them.

Concentrate on the images if you desire. In a few moments, prepare to share the images. Try to see them in their totality.

Be aware of your feelings and at the count of 3, 1-2-3 move some part of your body. Open your eyes.

Processing:

Share your images. Try to avoid interpretation. Report only what you have seen. Later on, you can go below the surface meanings for deeper meanings.

Digging for Ideas

DuPont was looking for new markets for its fire-resistant material used for protective clothing for firemen. It would have been ideal for airplane interiors, but the fabric was so tightly constructed, it would not hold dyes.

One DuPont scientist, who had been trained in creativity techniques, had grown up in West Virginia's coal country. He visualized the problem as a mine shaft. Miners dig a hole in the earth, and shore it up to keep it from collapsing. This metaphor inspired the scientist to come up with a way to chemically prop open a hole in the fibers as the material was manufactured, so that it could be filled by dyes.

It is essential that participants draw their own conclusions. The trainer serves as a guide, often stepping back when necessary. In facilitating this exercise and the processing, it is important for you to remind the participants that if sensitive or damaging material emerges, it is permissible to keep these images private and that everyone will respect that desire.

Participants may share insights from the exercise in groups of three or four since most people are usually more comfortable sharing personal information and feelings in small groups. After 15 or more minutes, the leader can bring the whole group together by posing a question such as, "Were you surprised by anything?" or "Did anything become clearer?"

These open-ended questions encourage participants to share insights. The leader can then point out similarities and differences in the responses and reinforce the notion that different points of view provide new ideas and ways of looking at things. Also, it is important for the leader to stress that an understanding of one's self sets the stage for understanding others and applying creativity.

Step 6: Bridging from Internal to External

Images move from the interior landscape to an external, concrete experience. The following exercise will aid this process. (As with most visual imagery exercises, this one should be preceded by a relaxation exercise.) Instruct participants to:

> Close your eyes and listen to the instructions for the exercise.

It is important for the leader to pause after each image to allow time for inner seeing.

> Now that you are in a relaxed state, focus your awareness on your country. But as you picture it, observe that you are visiting before it was created as a nation.

> What you see now is the land many years ago, before Europeans settled here (for America). To see it fully, you must float above it, lightly as a bird.

> Look about you and observe the land itself.

(Pause after each of the following questions to give sufficient time for silent reflection.)

- What do you see?
- What does the land look like?
- Are there trees? Rivers? Mountains? Deserts?
- What else do you see?
- Are there animals?
- Are there people?
- How do they look?
- What are they wearing?
- What do you notice about their appearance—hands, hair, eyes, height?
- What are they doing?
- Are they working?
- Caring for families?
- Do they seem happy? Sad? Serious? Lighthearted?
- What might these people be thinking about?
- What might they worry about?

When you are ready, open your eyes. Shift in your chair and reflect quietly on how you feel and what you now know.

Processing: As suggested with the previous exercise, the participants can share insights in small groups. The following questions are helpful:

- Would anyone like to describe what they saw? (land, people, etc.)
- What were people doing? Feeling?
- How did you feel going through this exercise?
- What did you realize?

Record the group's comments on a flipchart and use this information later in problem solving or as an introduction to other exercises. This exercise can be used to create a base for exercises in customer awareness to understand how people you deal with view a situation. One example:

Fishing for Ideas

A group of FritoLay employees were looking for a name for a new Frito cheese product. Creativity trainer Bryan Mattimore led the group on an imaginary trip to the South Pacific in a fishing boat. The imagined trip and the idea of fishing helped the group come up with the name "Great White Cheddar."

Provide the group adequate time to discuss the experiences and ideas and then ask for feedback from individual groups. You can conclude this exercise by providing opportunities for participants to brainstorm preliminary ideas that may apply to a problem being considered.

This visual imagery exercise provides a wealth of material and insights. Useful questions include:

- What in the situations you saw could be applied to your circumstances?
- What did you notice about the worries of the people that were peculiar to their time or situation? How do these apply to your situation?
- Would people from other countries be likely to have the same concerns? What would be different for you?

Resistance and Pitfalls

Group participants are often resistant to any type of interactive training activities. It is possible that some participants may be puzzled or fearful of the use of guided imagery.

This reaction is understandable, especially if they cannot see the connection to other learning tools and techniques. Resistance diminishes somewhat when you point out that visual imagery can be used as a type of quick problem solving. It also is helpful to reframe the activity to emphasize its usefulness for a specific group and to use conventional language to explain visual imagery. In each case, share the

Fantastic Voyage

Managers at Texas Utilities were charged with the task of reducing capital equipment costs. The managers used visualization and imagined themselves as kilowatts traveling through the company's systems.

They used this process over several months and traveled slowly throughout the entire system. They emerged with a greater understanding of the intricacies of the system. As a result, the managers came up with a new maintenance plan, focusing on replacing only subparts of the total system, that will reduce capital equipment costs tenfold over the next ten years.

—*Technology Review*

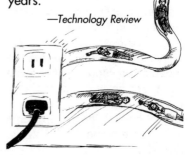

rationale behind the activity, and always give individuals the choice to participate or abstain.

Participants may need help in understanding the value of visual imagery. Point out that visual imagery enhances role-playing, simulation, problem-solving exercises, and group creativity. Success in most endeavors may be increased if participants are given opportunities to rehearse by imaging different roles, ideas, and attitudes. Remind them that the risk is minimal since one is only imagining these different ways of being.

Other participants may be uncomfortable with the ambiguity or open-endedness of visual imagery exercises. It is important that the use of imagery be distinctly related to the training goals of the program and clearly guided by the facilitator or trainer.

Later, when participants are more comfortable with the tool and accustomed to using visual imagery, you can drop some of the guidance and encourage participants to create their own imagery. Visual imagery deepens interpersonal and intrapersonal understanding and is complementary to other methodologies. It heightens learning and aids in developing content for creativity case studies and role-plays.

> "Practice learning to think in pictures. The man who built the Brooklyn Bridge said that he visualized the whole thing before it was built."
> —Henry Miller

USING VISUAL IMAGERY FOR CREATIVITY

Rudolph Arnheim, philosopher and former professor of visual studies, investigated the relationship between thinking and seeing. He concluded that images acquired early in life usually support basic learning and give us the basis for moving to higher levels of reasoning. This conclusion leads us to appreciate how fundamental the use of imagery is in solving problems and engaging in creative thinking.

Creativity sessions are only one of the contexts in which visual imagery can be a powerful tool. Imagery exercises can also be tailored to specific individuals and groups to help them plan, prepare, and take responsibility for aspects of a new experience. Some uses of the exercises include:

- problem solving in specific settings
- goal setting
- creative workshops on overseas relocation and re-entry
- general cultural awareness
- values clarification
- preparing professionals to provide services for a specific group
- building empathy with customers
- orientation programs
- leadership development
- communication

> ## Drawing Visualizations
>
> Another technique is to have participants sketch their visualizations. Through the sharing of drawings, many responses can be stimulated. It's not necessary that participants be able to draw well—in fact, sketches by "nondrawers" in the group often elicit the most novel responses because other participants see different things than the artist intended!

Creative Problem Solving: Presentations

Here is an example of using visualization as a creative problem-solving tool.

In a session I ran with middle managers of a large company, a manager framed his problem as, "In what ways might I introduce a training session to make it more interesting?" He was placed in a group with two other individuals. The other managers asked several idea-finding questions such as: "How many people will be there?" "Is this a compulsory meeting?" "Is there usually much enthusiasm at these meetings?" "Do you get nervous when you present?" and "Have you given presentations before?"

At this point, the three managers were told to close their eyes and to visualize answers. They could capture the ideas if they desired on flipcharts, in notebooks, or trust their memories.

After several minutes, the managers shared their spontaneous images. One imagined the manager in a game setting, pitching the ball and playing quite vigorously. The other saw him standing before a group of people and opening a bag of surprises, with all eyes riveted on him. His own image was that of a magician pulling rabbits out of a hat.

The manager who identified the problem chose the image of a bag of surprises to work on and discussed the image with the other two managers. He decided to prepare a talk that would be full of surprises to get attention immediately, and to use different approaches. After the training the next day, the manager received feedback that the session had been unique and informative.

Creative Problem Solving: Confidence

In another group, two women managers and one man who was a trainer were engaged in problem solving using visualization. They chose to work on the problem of one of the women managers who was having difficulty dealing with a business problem because of an overriding personal problem. She worded her problem as, "In what ways might I become more socially confident?" The two other managers asked her questions such as: "Have you always felt socially uncomfortable?" "Are you married?" "Are you seeing other people now?" "Do you have any outside interests?" "Are you finding it difficult to trust others?"

When the three visualized the problem, one person saw the young woman manager as a medieval warrior in a suit of armor in a museum. As the image progressed, the manager took off the armor, leaving the lighter chain mail on, and playfully brandished a spear. Another person's image had her whirling with other people around a Maypole, spinning with the others and laughing. The third person's image was of her entering a bakery shop, then buying lots of good-smelling baked goods to share with others on the street.

She chose the image with the armor and the museum. She said that was how she felt; that she had built armor around herself and had been using a sword to keep people away. She decided to take off some of the armor and brandish her spear (her strengths) and approach others with trust.

The young woman manager felt very comfortable with her interpretation of the image and was pleased that the group helped her solve her problem.

KEYS TO SUCCESSFUL VISUALIZATION

Clarity and specificity are necessary for the success of a creative visualization. A successful visualization should meet these criteria:

- It must interest the participant(s).
- The participants must have the knowledge to develop visual pictures of the situation.
- Multiple senses should be "visualized"
- any language used should be specific and unambiguous.
- You should visualize success, not failure.

> ### Time-Track Visualization
>
> In this technique, the individual or group imagines the end of the training session, or the day, or a project that has gone extremely well. Reflecting on the imagined past ("What I liked about my day was the way we really worked as a team") is a way to visualize the future.

Visualization is a way to tap the creative power of your right brain. Studies in the *Journal of Mental Imagery* showed that the more training you have, the better your visualization ability becomes. As you develop ways to express yourself visually, you'll have the benefit of your own "whole brain" approach to creativity. (See also Chapters 1 and 2.)

CONCLUSION

Visualization can be used in many ways as a creativity and innovation tool. For instance, many images can be seen as symbolic. They can become creativity stimuli as you free associate how they might apply to a problem. Sharing images also gives others something to react to in helping you solve your problem.

Visual imagery can also be used as visual brainstorming in regular brainstorming sessions. (See Chapter 5 for more discussion of brainstorming.)

Like any skill, visualization ability gets better with practice. With practice, you will be able to maximize your use of this valuable technique for creative applications.

ACTION SUMMARY

"Seeing opportunity and seizing it are two different things."
—Grover Cleveland

- Practice shutting your eyes and using visualizations to take a fresh look at problems you need new solutions for.

- Use creative visualization to imagine how another type of person would solve a problem, perhaps someone from another time period or culture.

- Practice the difference between visualizing a specific situation (dharana) and adding movements as when role-playing (dhyana).

- Experiment with using a visual "mandala" to help you focus your mind and relax.

- Develop a relaxation exercise to help you go into a more creative state.

- Experiment with music to help you feel creative. Classical baroque is supposed to stimulate alpha states—relaxation states that have been shown to enhance creativity.

- List other areas where creative visualization could help you, such as goal setting, communication, or values clarification.

Chapter 7

OPEN THE WINDOWS OF YOUR MIND...
Use the Power of Reframing to Produce Creative Ideas

Deanna H. Berg

Deanna H. Berg,
EdD, is president of Innovation Strategies International, a consulting firm known for its unique approaches to the critical areas of innovation, change, and teamwork.

Dr. Berg has facilitated the improvement efforts of many organizations worldwide such as Ford, NASA, Southwest Airlines, Xerox, and Lucent Technologies. She is a recognized expert in creative learning strategies and combines psychology with extensive corporate experience to move people beyond their accustomed ways of thinking. She earned her doctorate in counseling psychology and business from Indiana University.

Dr. Berg is a published author and member of the World Future Society, the Association of Quality and Participation, the American Society of Training and Development, Meeting Planners International, The Society for Organizational Learning, and the National Speakers Association. She is on the board of the Innovation Network, is an associate of The Learning Circle, a Boston-based network of leading thinkers and practitioners in the area of learning organizations, and works extensively with Create-It™, a global creativity consulting firm.

Deanna H. Berg, Innovation Strategies International, 5196 Corners Drive, Atlanta, GA 30338; phone (770) 351-5080 or (800) 660-9818; fax (770) 351-5081; e-mail deanna@profitplay.com; Web site www.profitplay.com.

Chapter 7

OPEN THE WINDOWS OF YOUR MIND...
Use the Power of Reframing to Produce Creative Ideas

Deanna H. Berg

"Our old views constrain us. They deprive us from engaging fully with this universe of potentialities."
—Margaret Wheatley

Mindsets—fixed mental frameworks—hamper our natural abilities to view problems in new ways and expand our solution possibilities. In his book, *Orbiting the Giant Hairball*, creativity expert Gordon MacKenzie describes how every new business decision or policy becomes part of a "hairball" dedicated to past realities, with no room for original thinking.

These hairballs, or frames, function all of the time, both consciously and unconsciously. They constrain our actions so that we see only what we want or expect to see.

The inability to see creative options is a major reason why so many organizations find it difficult to make and sustain desired changes. Making decisions from a limited range of possibilities leads to poor track records in improvement. Entrenched beliefs and actions determine both degree of organizational agility as well as effectiveness of business transformation.

Limited or distorted frames of reference lead individuals, work teams, and entire organizations to operate at far less than their maximum capabilities. This, in turn, leads to low morale, decreased profits, and even business failure.

"Reframing" is a powerful way to override our natural inclination to force-fit reality into preconceived mental models. It allows consideration of potentially valuable ideas outside of our current frames or "belief boxes."

WHAT IS REFRAMING?

"Reframing is the ability to see things, problems, situations or people in other ways, to look at them sideways or upside-down; to put them in another perspective or context; to think of them as opportunities not problems, as hiccups rather than disasters."

—Charles Handy, *The Age of Unreason*

Our perceptions and reactions to events are based on our past experiences. But, our past success strategies may actually work against us in the future.

As we grow and become "educated," we often put an unconscious frame around things we think we can or should do. Options that exist beyond our personal frame are not allowed into our awareness. Just as a picture frame encloses a picture, this in-

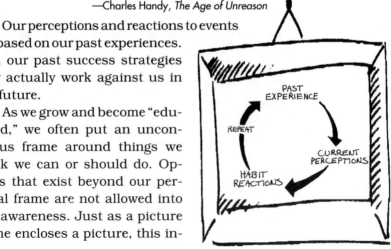

visible frame controls the ideas we see as appropriate or desirable. We fall into the trap of assuming tomorrow's experiences will be similar to those we have experienced in the past. This assumption impairs our ability to imagine breakthrough ideas.

BARRIERS TO REFRAMING

"We don't see things as they are, we see them as we are."

—Anais Nin, American author

Our frames are not wrong—just limiting and misleading. Without an awareness of all our options, we habitually do more of what we've done before—even when our actions don't get us the outcomes we want. We operate out of mental prisons because we can't look at our problems in new ways. Several common habits limit our ability to change mental frames (see box at left).

The Most Common Habits That Limit Our Ability to Change Mental Frames

Pursuit of perfection—we waste a great deal of energy trying to preserve the illusion we have everything under control and that we will find the perfect answer if we just work long enough or hard enough.

Fear of failure—We don't change because we don't want to risk looking incompetent, dumb, or foolish.

Delusion of already knowing the answer—We make "premature cognitive commitments" and stop looking for new options. We see no reason to change anything.

Terminal seriousness—We don't make opportunities to use our playful curiosity and humor to gain an expanded vision of what's possible.

WAYS REFRAMING INCREASES CREATIVE SUCCESS

"Problems cannot be solved by thinking within the framework in which the problems were created."

—Albert Einstein

Use reframing strategies when you aren't getting the results you want. The whole picture changes when we put a new frame around it. Central to these reframing strategies is the idea that changing the way we think will change our perceptions and behavior.

Changes in any of these variables alter the choices we see available. The problem is that a particular frame may be incomplete or distorted. If we aren't aware of this, we may assume we have the entire picture, and then be disappointed when our outcomes are less than ideal.

Our framing assumptions are valuable points of reference, but should be viewed only as opinions, not the *ultimate* truth. Reframing doesn't necessarily generate new options, but the ability to change our frames or step outside them, helps us discover alternatives that have always been there.

Limiting Frames

Some frames limit us more than others. Two frames that inhibit solution-finding abilities are:

Pessimistic Frame. If our frames are mostly negative, we are afraid to engage in new experiences that could lead to the discovery of new ideas. When we perceive our ideas as defective or inadequate and anticipate a negative future, we don't invest the time and energy needed to change perspectives.

Expert Frame. As we become more experienced in a particular area, we find that we know more and more about less and less; our frames of reference become smaller. If we believe strongly we are "right," we distort data to make it fit our frame. We miss the impact of other peoples' new ideas because we are busy listening to our own internal ideas.

As experts, our minds are so full of infor-

Variables to Consider When Reframing

Size. How large or small is our frame? This determines the number of options we perceive in a specific situation.

Thickness. How easy or difficult is it for new ideas to enter our frame? This determines our degree of openness or resistance to change.

Type. How positive or negative is our frame? This greatly influences the types of options we see in any situation.

Flexibility. How easy is it for us to change the way we frame our experiences? This affects our ability to gain new perspectives by viewing a given situation from several different frames.

Ownership. Whose frame of reference is it? Use multiple frames to achieve multiple perspectives.

mation, we are enable to engage in what management consultant Robert Greenleaf calls "bare listening." When we have used the same frame for so long, it's difficult to understand how anyone could possibly see things differently. Our expert opinion—based on past and present experiences—may have little value in predicting the future. In the words of management guru Peter Drucker, "we slaughter tomorrow's opportunities on the altar of yesterday."

Viewing situations from frames different from our normal ones empowers us to go beyond our own "obstinate obvious," as Gordon MacKenzie calls the reality created by our social conditioning.

TEN WAYS TO FRAME REALITY

You can view a problem through different frames to trigger original ideas. Following are ten ways you can reframe your experiences to create a new context for creative ideas.

Opportunity Frame

"Now that my house has burned down, I have a much better view of the sky."

—Zen master

We usually see the benefits of negative situations only after the negative situation has passed. This frame can help us achieve that same perspective without having to wait so long. This frame illuminates the hidden opportunities in difficult situations. Temporarily put aside the negatives of your "house burning down" and look at the new possibilities. As the late motivational expert Dr. Norman Vincent Peale used to say, every opportunity comes wrapped in a problem.

Flex Frame

> "There is nothing either good or bad, but thinking makes it so."
> —William Shakespeare

We can flex our frames by changing size, color, shape, material, etc. The more we do this, the greater number of ideas we generate. Another variation is to reframe one word or element of the problem at a time. View your situation from a variety of frames (for example, pessimistic/optimistic/neutral) and examine the opportunities and pitfalls made visible by each viewpoint. For example, one management team practices looking at problems through both *rose-colored* (positive) and *manure-colored* glasses (negative).

Or, use the *Five/Fifteen/Fifty* Frame to increase the number of ideas available to explore. First, think of options in response to a specific question. Then generate 15 more ideas and finally 50 new ideas. Or, after generating the first five ideas, choose the one you like best; then think of 15 variations or aspects of the selected idea, and 50 ideas related to one of the 15. This process forces your frames to expand.

Future Frame

> "If we don't change our direction, we're likely to end up where we're headed."
> —Chinese proverb

When you think of your company's (or your own) future, what thoughts come to mind? How would you complete the following sentence: *"By the year 2010, my company will be_____."* If you

> "Habit #2: Start with the end in mind."
>
> —Stephen Covey, *Seven Habits of Highly Effective People*

don't like what you wrote in the blank, what can you do now to change it? If you do like your prediction, what can you do to make sure it happens?

Envision conditions five or ten years in the future and imagine what new options have arisen. Think about all the things that might be different. Read the predictions of noted futurists and discuss the implications for your company if even the most unbelievable ones were to come true. Use scenario-planning activities, such as those described by Peter Schwartz in *The Art of the Long View*, to help imagine ideas for future possibilities.

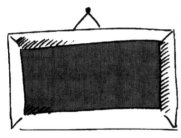

Failure Frame

> "I make more mistakes than anyone else I know and sooner or later I patent most of them."
>
> —Thomas Edison

Nothing inspires new ideas more quickly than an environment where people are free to take risks. For ideas to flow freely, we need to open ourselves to being wrong. When was the last time you took a risk? When was your last good mistake? Ask yourself, "What would be the best way to fail in this situation?" or "What is the worst thing we might do to try to improve this situation?" Then reverse those ideas to generate possible solution strategies. Or imagine worst-case scenarios—describe three or more ways the problem could be worse, or the absolute worst possible solution to the situation.

> "Tolerance for failure is a very specific part of the excellent company culture. Champions have to make of lot of tries and consequently suffer some failures or the organization won't learn."
>
> —Peters and Waterman, *In Search of Excellence*

To embrace failure as an investment in learning, we must give up perfectionism and relinquish our desire to keep everything under control. According to psychologist Dr. Janet Lapp, flexibility and *failing forward faster* are keys to thriving in times of unpredictable change.

Fun Frame

"A person might be able to play without being creative...but sure can't be creative without playing."

—Kurt Hanks & Jay Parry,
Wake Up Your Creative Genius

The fun/play/joy frame liberates creative ideas by reducing stress and creating the preconception-free perspective necessary for successful decision making. Play allows us to experiment and stretch ourselves without fear of negative consequences. Having fun with others is a powerful source of invention because it opens us to diverse views and allows us to experiment with new possibilities.

The predominant belief used to be that work and play should be separate. The new frame is that we can have fun and still get results. And, in the process, we might even create a company where people want to come to work!

CEO Jack Stack accomplished this at Springfield Remanufacturing Corporation by reframing business into a game and inspiring people to play it. Southwest Airlines makes it easy for both employees and customers to engage in creative, fun breaks. Often, these breaks lead to laughter and "a new lens" or frame through which they can view a particular situation, problem, or task.

Fun is largely a state of mind, so any activity can be done playfully—relax the rules to explore alternatives and expand beyond limiting mindsets. For maximum creative capacity, plan more playtime into your life.

"Having a ball is important for you and your people. It's one of the major rewards of playing the game."

—Jack Stack, *The Great Game of Business*

Friends-and-Family Frame

"Many ideas grow better when transplanted into another mind than in the one where they sprang up."

—Oliver Wendell Holmes

To realize the full power of reframing, it's helpful to view situ-

ations through frames that are different from our own. When we're open enough to elicit and accept the validity of others' ideas, we don't need as much flexibility in seeing things from many perspectives ourselves. Ask friends, family members, and co-workers who differ most from you how they see a particular situation. Or, imagine how these people would approach a situation and record the ideas that emerge.

Other viewpoints help us recognize unexpected opportunities. Innovative ideas are more likely to arise from diverse perspectives. What insights might be achieved by viewing a problem through the eyes of our customers? A child? A weird friend? A Zen master? Some innovation teams ensure the maximum variety of views by including members from other companies (in unrelated industries), or even other countries, to provide fresh perspectives.

Fame Frame

"The answer to any problem pre-exists. We need to ask the right question to reveal the answer."

—Jonas Salk

This is a variation of the *Friends-and-Family Frame*. In the Fame Frame, you imagine how different famous people might deal with a situation. These famous people can be real or imaginary; living or dead. Choose people about whom you know enough to guess the suggestions they might provide. (You can even call or write famous people to get their opinions. If you do, be sure you give some benefit or reason they should take time to respond.)

Consider television and movie stars, historical figures, celebrities, sports figures, philosophers, politicians, psychologists, media personalities, and business people as your personal consultants.

Fantasy Frame

"Imagination is the beginning of creation."
—George Bernard Shaw

Use this frame when you want to generate the most unconventional ideas. Fantasy involves a "belief bypass" to create as much distance as possible between what is now and what might be. Go to extremes. Ask *what if* questions such as:

- What might we do if we had unlimited funds?
- What might happen if price were no longer a factor in customer decisions?
- What seems impossible for us to do and what might happen if our competitors did it?

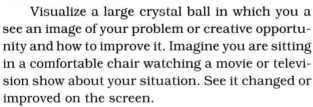

Use guided fantasies to imagine you are the object, process, problem, or opportunity you are considering. How do you feel? What caused you? How can you change yourself? Fantasize your problem as an animal, plant, song, machine, flower, city, or other unrelated object, process, or context and see what new ideas come forth.

Visualize a large crystal ball in which you a see an image of your problem or creative opportunity and how to improve it. Imagine you are sitting in a comfortable chair watching a movie or television show about your situation. See it changed or improved on the screen.

Imagine exploring your problem with all the openness, adventurousness, and curiosity you had as a child. Pretend to have a magic wand or Aladdin's Lamp with a genie who provides you with fantasy solutions to the problem. Make up other contexts to connect with your problem—anything goes in the *Fantasy Frame*!

Fiction Frame

"People live, reason and are moved by stories and symbols."

—Tom Peters

Stories stimulate new levels of awareness and creative behavior, often at the subconscious level. Stories inspire us to suspend old rules and forge new linkages among previously unconnected ideas and objects. They act as metaphors and analogies. They bypass conscious scripts and resistance, to help us step out of current reality and entertain new possibilities.

For example, use a *Detective Frame* (Colombo, Sherlock Holmes, Dick Tracy, etc.) and reproduce a famous sleuth's approach to problems.

Who is your favorite fictional character? What was your favorite fairy tale when you were a child? Books such as *Sherlock Holmes, Curious George, Tom Sawyer, The Little Engine That Could,* and *Robin Hood* help us suspend certainty, to go beyond our usual frame of reference and tap our unconscious resources.

Ask yourself how these characters would answer the questions you're considering. Or, tell a story about your problem, situation, or company and create multiple endings.

You might also combine the *Fiction Frame* with the *Fame Frame* and make up stories about how an expert might resolve the problem.

Flip-Side Frame

"Every exit is an entry somewhere else."

—Tom Stoppard, playwright

Use the *Flip-side Frame* to create new problem-solving mindsets. For example, if you want to improve customer service at your company, brainstorm for two minutes all the possible ways you could make customer service worse. This frame helps us break old rules that were valuable in the past, but now serve as anchors that prevent us from sailing to new horizons.

Practice this frame by listing the most obvious "truths" about your problem or challenge, then reverse them. Imagine as many opposites as you can and think about how they could also be true. Rotate the frame to look at the problem upside down—generate unlikely and outrageous ideas.

> ### A New Perspective
>
> A Minnesota company had a "Backwards Day" where employees dressed, walked, and talked backward. This experience served as a reminder not to assume things have to continue to be the way they've always been.

A REFRAMING GUIDE

Be curious and ask frame-breaking questions about every aspect of the target situation. For example: *What features taken for granted in our industry should we reduce, eliminate or raise to higher levels? What might we create that no one in our industry has ever offered?*

The reality we see depends on the questions we ask, so question all usual assumptions about things that are taken for granted about the challenge you are investigating.

With practice you can learn to change frames whenever you want to expand boundaries and provide a playground for new ideas. Changing frames doesn't mean you give up frames that have served you in the past. You simply extend and build on past learning to discover previously invisible options.

> ### If At First You Don't Succeed...
>
> If all else fails to trigger unique ideas, imagine your frames with holes in them so ideas can flow through freely; or, even better, imagine that you have *no* frames; you are open to any possibility. Consider options that appear to be totally outside the frame—that you believe are absolutely impossible.
>
> What might happen if you found a way to do them?

Reframing Outline

The following outline can help you practice reframing:

Step One: Select a current situation that you consider to be undesirable or unpleasant. Describe it briefly:

_____

_____

_____

Step Two: Determine if the situation is:
- *Avoidable or under your control?* If so, take action to avoid or control it.
- *Unsure?* Get additional information (this usually involves talking with someone else).
- *Unavoidable or out of your control?* Go to Step Three to change your perspective and find additional options.

Step Three: Reframe. Apply any of the frames described earlier, or others you select or create. Do this as often as needed in order to generate enough new ideas to evaluate for potential implementation.

_____

_____

_____

Step Four: Try altering or combining ideas from your pool. Apply reframing techniques such as reversing to these new ideas.

Step Five: Evaluate the ideas you come up with and choose those that warrant further development. Do NOT evaluate until this step.

CONCLUSION

"If things seem under control, you're just not going fast enough."

—Mario Andretti

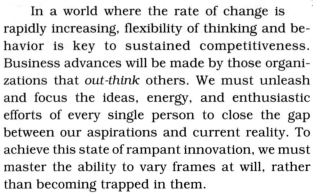

In a world where the rate of change is rapidly increasing, flexibility of thinking and behavior is key to sustained competitiveness. Business advances will be made by those organizations that *out-think* others. We must unleash and focus the ideas, energy, and enthusiastic efforts of every single person to close the gap between our aspirations and current reality. To achieve this state of rampant innovation, we must master the ability to vary frames at will, rather than becoming trapped in them.

To maximize opportunities to learn, reframe the learning process itself. Reframe all situations—successes and failures—as learning

---

Thinking, Ideas, and Information
by Edward de Bono

Information may trigger ideas, which may trigger an information search. Information does not easily yield up all the ideas that are present in that information. The mind has to put things together in different ways—to generate possibilities and even provocations. Sometimes there is information which everyone has looked at in a particular way. Then someone comes along and uses lateral thinking to look at information in a different way and reaches a new hypothesis about it.

It is a mistake to believe that collecting enough information will do all our thinking for us. Information is not a substitute for ideas and thinking. On the other hand, there is a real need for information. The key is to sustain an active interplay between thinking and information collecting. Thinking directs information collecting and also makes the best use of what has been collected. At the same time information may suggest ideas, confirm some ideas, and lead to the rejection of others.

opportunities. Realize that formal training is not always the most effective way to learn. Learning is an ongoing process, not a one-time event. Provide a structure for people to learn while they work. Give people time to think, reflect, and plan. After each new experience, take time to reflect on what worked and what didn't. Ask yourself what you would do differently the next time.

People who master reframing report a liberating sense of choice and the power to develop new alternatives. Reframing enables creative discovery of options that are invisible to us when viewed with our old frames. Imagine how much we would accomplish if—instead of reusing the same worn-out ideas—everyone were fully aware of all available possibilities and constantly refilling "option shelves."

ACTION SUMMARY

"Procrastination is opportunity's natural assassin!"
—Victor Kiam

- When negative things happen, look for the new opportunities opened up.

- Change a series of aspects of the situation to find new perspectives.

- Look at the future of a situation and imagine how you could change it.

- Thomas Edison said that the fastest way to increase your success was to double your failure rate. Give yourself permission to fail and imagine ways to fail for new perspectives.

- Stretch your view by playing with a situation.

- Ask other people who are different from you for fresh perspectives.
- Imagine how famous people would handle a situation.
- Imagine extreme fantasy situations for new insights.
- Make up a story about your situation, or adapt a story like *Tom Sawyer*.
- List your own frames of reference, and reverse them for fresh perspectives.

Chapter 8

HOW TO INCREASE YOUR CREATIVE BRAINPOWER

Joan E. Cassidy

Joan E. Cassidy,
EdD, is founder and president
of Integrated Leadership Concepts, Inc., and a quality man-
agement consultant, educator, speaker, and author. Since 1974, she has
assisted dozens of public and private sector organizations and trained thousands
of managers and their employees to improve the quality of their products and
services. She attributes her success to her ability to "walk and talk" in all four
quadrants of the "whole brain model."

Dr. Cassidy consults and speaks nationally and internationally with *Fortune*
100 and *Fortune* 500 companies. She also hosts her own cable television
program dedicated to exploring business issues across many levels of the
organization.

In addition, Dr. Cassidy teaches graduate level courses at National Louis
University and has previously taught graduate level courses in total quality
management (TQM) at Virginia Polytechnic Institute and State University, and
Marymount University where she developed a TQM certification program. In
1994, Dr. Cassidy was named "Distinguished Consultant in Quality" in the
International Who's Who in Quality.

Dr. Joan E. Cassidy, Integrated Leadership Concepts, Inc., P.O. Box 523080,
Springfield, VA 22152; phone (703) 866-1184; fax (703) 866-7931; e-mail
ilcinc@aol.com; Web site www.ilconcepts.com.

Chapter 8

HOW TO INCREASE YOUR CREATIVE BRAINPOWER

Joan E. Cassidy

"Ideas are like rabbits. You get a couple and learn how to handle them, and pretty soon you have a dozen."

—John Steinbeck

Einstein is reputed to have said that the average person only uses about 10 percent of his or her brainpower. Imagine what you could do if you could double that figure to 20 percent. You could become 100 percent more innovative, 100 percent smarter!

I am not going to promise that you will become 100 percent more effective or 100 percent smarter if you read this chapter. But, the more you understand and apply the information here, the more you increase your odds of success.

A BRIEF OVERVIEW

Throughout history, humans have been trying to understand how the brain works. As early as 450 BC, Hippocrates wondered why injuries to the left side of the head usually resulted in impaired functions on the right side of the body and vice versa. In 1286, Roger Bacon described two ways of obtaining information or knowledge. The first was verbally, the other through experience.

Almost 600 hundred years later, a medical doctor, John Jackson, wrote about the notion of "brain dominance." He suggested that, for most people, one side of the brain tended to be dominant. Then, in the early 1970s, Roger Sperry's Nobel Prize-winning split-brain research dramatically added to what we knew about how the brain functions.

Left/Right Brain Dominance	
Left Side	**Right Side**
• Logical	• Non-Verbal
• Analytical	• Ideation
• Mathematical	• Holistic
• Linear	• Synthesizing
• Sequential	• Simultaneous

Since then, hundreds of other researchers around the world have developed additional experimental techniques to locate, identify, and measure the degree to which mental capabilities are controlled by one hemisphere or the other. One of those researchers was Ned Herrmann, recognized internationally as the "Father of Brain Dominance Technology."

The Herrmann Quadrants

In his early research, Herrmann discovered that the data he was collecting did not neatly fit into just left- or right-brain categories. Rather, he noticed that four categories emerged. As a result, he developed a metaphorical model of the brain that consisted of four quadrants. He later constructed the Herrmann Brain Dominance Instrument (HBDI), a 120-item self-administered questionnaire that is scored by professionals trained in

Brain Quadrants

UPPER LEFT	UPPER RIGHT
(Analytical)	**(Experimental)**
logical	holistic
quantitative	intuitive
fact-based	synthesizing
	integrating

LOWER LEFT	LOWER RIGHT
(Organizational)	**(Interpersonal)**
planned	emotional
organized	feeling-based
detailed	kinesthetic
sequential	

brain dominance concepts. The instrument provides a valid, reliable measure of mental preferences.

To date, Herrmann has collected millions of samples to demonstrate individual preferences. His research shows that everyone has a unique mix of mental preferences and avoidances. However, most people tend to have at least one dominant, or preferred quadrant with a supporting secondary quadrant. Preferences for the remaining quadrants vary depending on the strength of the primary and secondary quadrants. In some cases, the least preferred quadrant may be so weak, it can be characterized as an "avoidance."

Left- versus Right-Brain Characteristics

Considerable research has shown that many top executives, managers, and supervisors tend to have preferences that are strongly left-oriented (logical, analytical, quantitative, fact-based, planned, organized, detailed, sequential). As a result, most organizations tend to focus on activities that are primarily left-brain-oriented.

Right-brained activities (holistic, intuitive, synthesizing, integrating, emotional, interpersonal, feeling-based and kinesthetic) are engaged in less frequently—or mostly avoided. Likewise, individuals who are more right-brain-oriented tend to be undervalued in organizations and, thus, underused.

What are the implications of this? When an organization focuses mostly on left-brain activities, at best it is functioning at 50 percent of its capacity! (And possibly even less.) Organizations that do not value and use right-brain activities tend to be very bureaucratic. Their focus is more on operational activities that are not necessarily connected to the big picture. There is not a great deal of employee involvement, nor is there a focus on the customer.

Balance Needed

My experience has taught me that when a manager or supervisor has an avoidance area for the lower-right quadrant (emotional, interpersonal, feeling based, kinesthetic), then he or she is not a good communicator. Managers and supervisors who are not good communicators often negatively impact the efficiency and effectiveness of the organization.

As an "Organization Doctor," my challenge often revolves around how to help managers, supervisors, and their employees become more efficient and effective.

Many years ago, after being certified by Ned Herrmann to use his instrument, I began to develop my own adaptation of his theories. I call it *Integrated-Brain Technology* and use it to transform organizations.

First, I administer the instrument to help people understand their own preferences and avoidance areas. Next, I perform a gap analysis to identify where they currently are versus where they need to be. I then focus on the key behaviors associated with obtaining desired results; develop

Supervisors' Communication Styles Affect Employees

Subordinates who rated their supervisors' communication styles as "affirming" were more committed to the organization, more satisfied with their superiors, and more satisfied with their work. Affirming communication is relaxed, friendly, and attentive, with low verbal aggressiveness. Verbally aggressive superiors were the most disliked. However, supervisors with affirming communications styles and who were high in argumentativeness, were rated highest by subordinates. These supervisors may be open to discussion.

—Infante & Gorden,
Western Journal of Communication

strategies to help them engage in those key behaviors; measure how well they are performing; and take appropriate actions to reward or improve less than desirable behaviors. When individuals learn the power of Integrated-Brain Technology, they learn to function more efficiently and more effectively. Let me give you an example.

A CASE STUDY

Several years ago, I was working with a large Federal government client. One of the managers supervised a staff of eight individuals who functioned as facilitators for Quality Improvement Problem Solving Teams. In one of our meetings, the manager expressed concern about her group. She explained that she had inherited a diverse group of individuals and was expected to improve the services they provided.

What Makes a Good Facilitator

The manager was stymied because these eight facilitators did not work well together. Furthermore, she had received numerous complaints that the differing styles of these facilitators confused the teams they were facilitating. She also indicated it was clear that some of the facilitators were more successful than others. She wasn't sure why, but wanted to find out. As we talked, she continued to wonder out loud about such things as,

- Is it possible that one style of facilitation is more successful than others? If so, is it possible to determine what contributes to success?
- Can we write it down?
- Can we look for people with these characteristics? Or, even better, can we train others so they can model the types of behaviors that are successful?

She was aware that I was in the process of identifying facilitator competencies in the organization and thought that Integrated-Brain Technology was a useful concept. She wanted to assess each member of her staff and determine whether or not they were suited for the role; and, if someone were not suited, she wanted to discuss alternatives.

I administered the instrument to all eight facilitators. To my surprise, no two individuals shared the same profile! Yet, the composite group profile reflected a "whole-brain" or a balanced distribution in the four quadrants. As I discussed these results with her, I became more excited. The possibilities were incredible!

According to the theory, *diversity* in thinking styles within a team or organization promotes *higher* levels of success. Yet her team verged on being dysfunctional. The reason for this was simple. Without an understanding of whole-brain technology and, without an attempt to implement it, the result is likely to be disharmony—with the potential for disaster!

A Five-Step Action Plan

In order to solve her problem, I suggested the following five-step approach:

1. Help individuals understand their own thinking styles, others' thinking styles, and the implications for differences and similarities.

2. Define successful facilitator competencies.

3. Conduct a gap analysis to determine the difference between existing individual competencies and desired competencies.

4. Develop specific strategies to close the gap.

5. Periodically check to see if actions are yielding desired results; if not, determine root cause(s) and take appropriate measures.

"Most companies don't fail for lack of talent or lack of strategic vision. They fail for lack of execution."
—T.J. Rodgers,
CEO, Cypress
Semiconductor

During the process, some of the facilitators recognized that they were ill-suited for their current roles. They asked for different assignments. Some individuals pinpointed deficiencies and developed action plans to improve their performance. Others were identified as role models to emulate.

Overall, we created win-win scenarios. The

manager achieved her goal—to improve facilitation services. Teams benefited because they were served by more competent facilitators. Finally, individuals were better aligned with their preferences and competencies, and were, therefore, better at what they did.

Square Pegs and Round Holes

The lesson to be learned here is that when managers and supervisors assign people to the wrong tasks, a breakdown in functioning results. In the case above, individuals were selected to be facilitators without any regard for whether they were suited for the role. The process was unsuccessful, despite the fact that most of them had really tried to perform.

One of the primary problems was that no one had clearly defined what the facilitators were supposed to do. Another was that when they finally learned what "facilitation" was all about, some did not have the requisite skills to perform.

In most organizations, managers and supervisors don't analyze what *specific* skills are required to perform various tasks. Without understanding what it takes to do a particular job, and without matching the right people with the right tasks, havoc results.

One of the first steps towards creating a Integrated-Brain Organization is to understand "who best wears which hats" and to align individuals with tasks. The next step is to help people learn to wear as many different hats as possible through developmental activities. Let's look at this in a little more detail.

Person-Environment Fit

$$P \times E = F$$

(where P = Person, E = Environment, and F = Fit)

In psychology, it has long been accepted that the interaction of the person and the environment will determine success. No one style or skill will fit all situations optimally.

—*Journal of Applied Psychology*

HOW TO CREATE AN INTEGRATED-BRAIN ORGANIZATION

In my consulting work, I focus on *results*. The greatest techniques and models are useless if people don't adjust their *behavior* to be consistent with desired results. The most expensive programs and training are worthless if people don't engage in appropriate *behaviors*. I am always amazed that managers don't seem to understand this concept. In the box at the right, I've illustrated this concept with a formula.

THE "VOWEL HATS" OF THINKING, COMMUNICATING, AND DECISION MAKING

As I said earlier, most people tend to favor certain modes of thinking, communicating, and decision making over others. Building on Herrmann's research, I have organized these modes of thinking, communicating, and decision-making into four categories:

> **A**nalytical
> **E**xperimental
> **I**nterpersonal
> **O**rganizational

Formula for Innovative Results

$$T \rightarrow S \rightarrow I \rightarrow F = R$$

T = Definition of the **T**ask(s)

S = Definition of the **S**kills required to perform tasks

I = Identification of **I**ndividuals who have the requisite skills or the ability to acquire skills through training/education

F = **F**eedback on how well people perform the task

R = **R**esults (What you want/ need/expect with respect to the tasks that individuals are performing)

Note that this formula indicates that each component must be done in a particular order.

Also note that the formula acronym TSIF is the word "fist" spelled backwards. Most organizations start with the "F" component—that is, they give their employees feedback without having defined the required tasks and skills, and without having identified the individuals appropriate to these tasks.

When companies do this process backwards—FIST—they're sucker-punched by a metaphorical fist. Despite any attempts to implement new programs, they don't get results.

That's A-E-I-O, which is then followed by You, where "You" represents the individual's recognition of the value of each category.

An organization needs to have people skilled in all four categories in order to make the transformation to high performance and creativity.

Less than five percent of the total population are able to perform well in all categories. Therefore, organizations need to learn to identify which skills are in each category and then ensure that they have people who have the representative skills. However, just having people with the skills is not enough. The final step requires that everyone recognize the value of each category and how to integrate the skills to create the optimal Integrated-Brain Organization.

DIFFERENT HATS FOR DIFFERENT PERSPECTIVES

Different types of hats can be used as a metaphor for different modes of thinking, communicating, and decision making. When people exercise their preferences, they tend to select the same one or two hats through which to perceive the world regardless of the situation. They also have trouble understanding others who aren't using the same hats. Let me give you an example:

"Genius means little more than the faculty of perceiving in an unhabitual way."
—William James

SCENARIO #1:
ORGANIZATIONAL VS. EXPERIMENTAL
Joe continuously has problems with his immediate supervisor, Mary. When Joe goes into a meeting with Mary, he is always prepared. He gives numerous examples of how he or others have always done things in the past. He feels good about the fact that things are stable and don't change a lot. He always has facts and figures to back up his position. Basically, we can say that Joe has a pragmatic view of the world and likes to work within the existing system.

(Joe's favorite hat is in the lower-left family.)

Mary was brought into the organization because the CEO felt that change was needed. She is viewed as a visionary and has been given a free hand to reorganize her department to take the company into the next millennium.

Mary views Joe as a dinosaur. She frequently becomes impatient with him because he doesn't seem to "get it." In this case, the "it" is the big picture. Mary does not care about the details Joe keeps presenting her. She wants to break out of the old way of doing things. She wants Joe to be more innovative and creative. In a recent meeting, she confided to the consultant, "If he tells me one more time, 'It ain't broke, so why mess with it!' I'm going to scream. Why can't he be more creative? I'm creative. I need people who think as I do if I am going to turn this company around!" (Mary prefers hats in the upper right family.)

Shades of George Bernard Shaw and Pygmalion! Remember Professor Henry Higgins' lament: "Why can't a woman be more like a man!" In this case, however, the woman wants the man to be more like her.

How about this scenario?

SCENARIO #2:
ANALYTICAL VS. INTERPERSONAL
Ralph has just had the latest of a continuing series of clashes with Harry, the team leader of his problem-solving team. He is more convinced than ever that Harry is a total flake.

This is the fourth team meeting and they still have not defined the problem. They have not established priorities. No financial data have been presented to establish the cost benefits. Ralph

> "New ways of thinking about familiar things can release new energies and make all manner of things possible."
> —Charles Handy

thinks they are just spinning their wheels needlessly. He has already researched the issue thoroughly and "knows" the answer. Why can't the others see it? After all, he is an expert in this field. He really doesn't see this team as going anywhere. (He is an upper-left quadrant thinker.)

Harry sees Ralph as an insensitive, pushy boor. Harry is concerned about what impact the issue at hand will have on the people in the organization. He has spent the first few meetings brainstorming, considering values, and trying to establish harmony in the group. He wants everyone to express how they *feel* about the issue before proceeding. His perception is that Ralph is not "into" this meeting because Ralph has never shown enthusiasm about anything. He just matter-of-factly continues to state his position and solution.

There was a particularly tense moment when Penelope, another team member, tried to make a point about the issue by sharing a personal example. Ralph became impatient with her and snapped, "Just stick to the facts." Even though Penelope said fine, Harry felt that she was upset by Ralph's comments because her body language later did not match her words—she became rigid (she was usually very relaxed and chatted easily) and did not speak for the rest of the meeting.

Harry made several attempts to reconcile the two, but to no avail. Ralph finally muttered, "This team reminds me of the Titanic....," and left the meeting. (Harry is lower-right quadrant.)

I am sure many of you can identify one or more situations in your own organizations where these scenarios are played out. In both cases, none of the participants grasped the underlying dynamics of the interactions because they didn't understand the concepts of Integrated-Brain Technology. And because they didn't, they were not as effective as they could have been.

APPRECIATING INDIVIDUAL DIFFERENCES

Let's fast forward to a point after the individuals have participated in a seminar to learn how to apply Integrated-Brain Technology concepts.

SCENARIO #1

Joe now rarely has problems with his immediate
supervisor, Mary, even though they have different
styles. Mary has come to value Joe's contributions to
the team. She lets him know that she values and
appreciates his thoroughness and attention to detail.
Joe, on the other hand, has learned when to introduce
pertinent examples to support the points he is trying
to make. While he is still more comfortable when
things don't change a lot or too quickly, he under-
stands that for the company to survive and thrive, it
must make changes. Mary now realizes that Joe's
pragmatic view of the
world is an asset and
often looks to him for
advice before moving
forward.

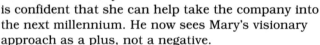

Joe also appreciates
Mary and recognizes
that the CEO made a
wise choice in Mary. Joe
is confident that she can help take the company into
the next millennium. He now sees Mary's visionary
approach as a plus, not a negative.

Both Mary and Joe have learned to value the
other's style. They now see that each company needs a
visionary, someone to focus on the future and work on
creative strategies to remain competitive (Mary, with
preferences for upper-right-brain activities). The
company also needs a healthy dose of pragmatism to
keep it grounded and focused on day-to-day operations (Joe, with preferences for lower-left-brain activities). Together, they make a powerful team, with each
one complementing the other's style.

SCENARIO #2

Ralph and Harry have finally come to a meeting of the
minds. Instead of continuously clashing with one
another, they have learned how to make their complementary styles more effective. Ralph has learned that
to go fast, you first have to go slow. Ralph now sees
the value of brainstorming, considering values, and
trying to establish harmony in the group. So, even
though he is anxious to get started—to "get down to

business"—he has learned to be patient during these first few meetings.

Harry now recognizes that some people view the above activities as "touchy-feely." He has worked hard to get everyone to understand why they must complete these types of activities first. At the same time, he has introduced some things of a more concrete nature so people like Harry can see immediate results. For example, he brings agendas and priorities to each meeting.

Ralph feels better about his participation because his teammates no longer view him as pushing his ideas down their throats. Conversely, the team members value Ralph's expertise.

Tense moments have all but disappeared. Penelope is very happy with the "new" way—Ralph even asks her for examples of how her personal experiences can help the team to move forward. Everyone agrees that the team is much more productive now that team members understand and appreciate each other's styles of communicating, thinking, and making decisions.

Right-Left Resolution

These examples demonstrate how a classic conflict between a right-brain orientation (Mary and Harry) and a left-brain orientation (Joe and Ralph) can be resolved. The conflict ceases to exist, or is at least put to constructive use, after individuals master the art of Integrated-Brain Technology.

Individuals learn that in a fully functioning organization, members must learn to wear many different hats. They also learn that some hats are more appropriate than others for some situations. They then learn to match individual styles and wear different hats to the appropriate occasions. In other words, they know when the situation calls for one of four types of hats:

- Analytical Scholar Hats
- Experimental Risk-Taking Hats
- Interpersonal Team Hats
- Organized Conservative Hats

Each category of hats reflects a distinct set of competencies, skills, and attitudes.

The Analytical Scholar Hat

Analytical scholar perspectives are useful for tasks that require concentrated thinking time alone, or for expressing oneself with confidence, firmness, or preciseness. This hat is also useful for the following types of activities:

- analyzing data
- explaining things (speaking and writing clearly and precisely)
- clarifying issues
- logical problem solving
- dealing with financial data
- focusing on the bottom line
- formulating theories or hypotheses

The Experimental, Risk-Taking Hat

Individuals who prefer the experimental risk-taking approach are usually some of the first to try out new ideas. They are always looking for ways that are better, cheaper, and faster. They are also good at seeing the "big picture" and "out-of-the-box thinking." They like to take risks and experiment.

The types of activities that require these skills include:

- inventing new solutions
- bringing about change
- designing a new approach
- selling a new idea
- developing a vision
- forecasting future activities

Whenever the situation requires a novel or fresh approach, people with this style are the first to suggest it may be appropriate to dispense with rules, or to brainstorm possibilities without imposing constraints.

The Interpersonal Team Hat

Managers and supervisors, as a group, tend to rarely use this hat. Even when they do use it, they do not wear it well. The types of activities in this category include:

- working together effectively as a team
- engaging in active listening
- "reading" body language and sensing what people are thinking
- negotiating win-win outcomes and mediating disagreements
- being helpful
- being customer oriented
- teaching or training
- coaching or counseling

People who prefer this hat are usually compassionate and understanding, and easily recognize what is important to others. They have learned not to assume what is meant or desired, but use good communication skills to ask questions and clarify wants, needs, and expectations.

The Organized, Conservative Hat

Organized conservative hats are best for activities that require sequencing or structuring, attention to detail, consistency, or being methodical and organized. People who prefer this hat are usually recognized as conservative, realistic, or dependable. Some examples of generic activities that would require one of these skills include:

- operational planning
- getting things done on schedule
- establishing order
- developing procedures and work instructions
- administrative activities or paperwork tasks
- organizing the physical environment
- bookkeeping
- data entry, word processing, and filing

- structuring tasks
- maintaining quality control
- preserving the status quo

BUILDING SELF-AWARENESS—
WHAT'S YOUR PREFERENCE?

It is important to understand the implications for each of your preferences for mental styles and types of activities. It is even more important to be aware of your strong avoidances for performing certain functions, for one or more of those functions may be critical to success.

The Integrated-Brain Technology Model

In order to ensure that you will be successful, use this five-step model:

1. Understand yourself (your preferences and thinking styles) and others (their preferences and thinking styles).

2. Define what constitutes success (critical competencies for what needs to be accomplished).

3. Conduct a gap analysis (the difference between where you currently are and where you need to be).

4. Take appropriate action (develop a plan to correct deficiencies, or do something else that better suits your profile).

5. Periodically check to see if actions are yielding desired results; if not, determine root cause(s) and make appropriate corrections.

It is rare for one individual to be able to wear all of the different hats well. However, if the desire exists, most individuals can be taught to compensate for most deficiencies. Still, others learn to fill

"Everyone is a genius at least once a year. The real geniuses simply have their bright ideas closer together."
—George Lichtenberg

the gaps by delegating or transferring activities that require skills they are unable or unwilling to master. A few discover that they are ill-suited and unmotivated to make the necessary changes. They then become liberated to pursue what they are better suited for and highly motivated to do.

How many different hats can *you* wear successfully?

ACTION SUMMARY

"An ounce of action is worth a tone of theory."

—Friedrich Engels

- Is your own preference more for the logical, organized (left brain) or holistic, interpersonal (right brain)?

- Within your left/right orientation, are you more: logical, analytical and quantitative (upper left) planned, organized, and detailed (lower left)

    or

    holistic, intuitive, integrating (upper right) emotional, interpersonal, kinesthetic (lower right)?

- Given your preferred style, what types of jobs do you enjoy most? What jobs should you not be doing?

- Jot down ways that you can work with each of the four styles.

- Choose a project for which you're responsible and check off which of the four types of perspectives would be useful in each stage.

Chapter 9

USING CREATIVITY IN THE SALES PROCESS
Step Out of Your Rut and Up to Success

Bill Blades

Bill Blades
is a consultant, speaker, and
author. At the age of 22, he
served as plant manager for a
major manufacturing firm while a full-time college student. Later, while serving as
vice president of sales and marketing for a food manufacturing concern, he
increased sales 150% from $13 million to $33 million in only four years. His firm
was named Small Business of the Year and was always the top marketing firm
in the food manufacturing area.

Mr. Blades is the author of the bestseller, *Selling: The Mother of all Enter-prise*. In addition, he is featured with noted attorney F. Lee Bailey in the book
Leadership Strategists.

One of only 51 Certified Management Consultants in the U.S. who speaks
and consults with clients in the areas of sales and marketing, Mr. Blades does
so with a straightforward mission statement: Our mission is to always deliver more
than we promise and to serve as our clients' partner in the quest for excellence.

Bill Blades, William Blades & Associates, Ltd., 11126 East Breathless Drive, Gold
Canyon, AZ 85219; phone (602) 671-3000; fax (602) 671-0926.

Chapter 9

USING CREATIVITY IN THE SALES PROCESS
Step Out of Your Rut and Up to Success

Bill Blades

"A rut is a grave without the ends filled in."
—Old folk saying

Some people might wonder, "Why a chapter on creativity in sales?" The answer is that sales is home to some of the most boring approaches you'll ever see. And, surprisingly, many salespeople not only bore their customers and prospects, but themselves as well!

Sales is the engine that drives the economy—and your business. It has a great need for applied creativity. You can't afford to *not* be creative in your sales approaches.

Creative approaches get results in every phase of the sales process, but are most frequently used to get attention and solve customer problems.

Any one approach won't work for everyone, and some of my examples may strike you as strange. Any time you're creative, you run the risk of being perceived as strange because you are deviant—you're out of the ordinary, not doing whatever everyone else is doing. The point is to put some creativity into your relationships with prospects and customers. You'll get more attention and you won't bore your customers and prospects—or yourself.

> ### Creative Ideas Rise Above Commodities
>
> Jack Ryel, a purchasing manager for Phillips 66 Company, finds his suppliers similar on quality and price. He looks for those who bring creative solutions with them. For instance, one salesperson came up with a new money-saving freight program that grouped loads through a third-party vendor.
> —*Sales & Marketing Executive Report*

YOU ADD UNIQUE VALUE

In sales, you can't succeed by "pushing stuff on people." You have to bring value to your relationships with prospects and customers. If they see your products or services as commodities, then *you* aren't contributing to the sale!

If you function merely as a conveyer of offers, as most salespeople do, you become a commodity—a salesperson who can be easily replaced by any other salesperson who comes along. You have to break out of the commodity mold. You are a unique person who no one else can duplicate.

You bring your own creative possibilities to each new relationship. It's your job to share them! This chapter will give you many examples of creative ideas in sales that you can adapt or implement.

ADD CREATIVE TOUCHES TO YOUR SALES CALLS

The sales process can be broken into a number of steps. Let's look at how creativity can come into play during the sales process.

Looking for Prospects

Before you meet with prospects, you have to find "suspects" (people who are likely to become prospects), do research, and prequalify people.

If you come up with ideas about possible "suspect" groups that others haven't considered, you will have new fields of prospects all to yourself. You might discover a new list or directory that others haven't used. Or your inspiration might come from a hobby that makes you a part of a group of possible prospects. Perhaps your shared interest group might become a source of referral leads that only you have.

The who-is-that-guy approach. Here's one unusual way I come up with prospects. When I walk through airports, I've got my "radar beam" out—I'm scanning to my left and right. I'm looking for all the discarded newspapers from different cities.

Then I glance through the papers, looking for items that either I or my clients can use. For example, I might read about a vice president of sales getting promoted. I'll have my staff locate this person's address and telephone number. Then I will send a card, usually without a business card: "Dear Fred, I read of your promotion. I'm sure you're well deserving. Congratulations. Sincerely, Bill." And at Fred's office, everyone's wondering, "Who in the heck is this Bill?" because Fred is in Rochester and I'm in Arizona.

Then I call. To the assistant who answers the phone, I say, "I dropped a note to Fred Jones, and I just wanted to call and again offer my congratulations." They often say, "*You're* that Bill who's been driving us crazy!"

I'm the first to admit that this is not rocket scientist stuff. But it's not *one* great big thing that

you do in life that's going to help you be successful—it's a series of small actions.

Making Your Initial Approach

The most creativity is needed in the initial
contact with prospects, but it's where the least is
generally used. Whether you're still trying to qualify
people, or fishing for appointments, the typical
approaches are boring for prospects and mechanical for salespeople.

The marketing formula AIDA stands for Attention, Interest, Desire, and Action. If you can't
get their attention and interest, no relationship
can develop—no matter how valuable the solutions you're selling. There's a crying need for
creativity here. Professional buyers have heard all
the standard approaches. These approaches are
worse than boring—they're insulting. The least
you can do is provide some entertaining novelty!

Stamp it creative. I've got my own "postage
stamps" with my picture on them. I race cars once
in awhile, and on the stamp I'm in my race car
outfit. Of course, the stamp has no monetary
value. What I do is hit the postage meter, and
then put my own stamp alongside the metered
postage. Before prospects have even opened the
envelope, I've gotten their attention. They're
saying, "What in the world? Look at this."

Year-round costume party. Robert
Stephens started a computer repair firm
that used "creativity in the absence of capital." His employees dress like 1950s' FBI
agents, have badges, and call themselves
the "Geek Squad." It gets attention. Simi-
larly, John Collins wears a green-and-
black caped costume and calls himself
"Toner Man" to promote his recondi-
tioned toner cartridges. After these service people appear at a business, you

SHOW SOME FLAIR
"Do whatever it
takes to get the
sale. Sometimes
that means going in
for show business
tactics."
—Ted Turner,
Turner
Broadcasting

can bet they're remembered. And they are asked back because when these service people show up, it's an event.

Out of the frying pan, into the sale. When one consultant finally reached a big prospect, the prospect said "I don't have time to talk to you. I have bigger fish to fry" and hung up. The consultant had a $22 frying pan delivered to the prospect's office the next day. The big prospect called, the two met, and a contract was signed.

The gong show. Here's another creative approach. When you promise a prospect that you will only take so much of his or her time without their permission to continue, bring an egg timer, a stopwatch, or even a gong to reassure the prospect that you really mean it. It also brings a smile and relaxes them.

"I told him that if he's not convinced to work with us after ten minutes, to just give us a signal."

Time is money. My own bias is to be a little "off the wall." I'd rather be thought too strange than too boring. You should be able to come up with creative approaches that fit your style.

Here's a simple way to grab attention. When it comes time to set up the first appointment with someone, the prospect might say, "Bill, can you come by next Thursday morning?"

"Love to. What time would be a great time for you?"

"Bill, come in anytime between 8 and 12."

"Great, I'd love to have the 8:03."

At this point, the prospect is likely taking the phone away from her ear, and looking at the phone, wondering, "What kind of screwball is this?" What I have done is to set it up from the very beginning that I am different from everybody else. Then I drop a confirming card: "Dear Elizabeth: It was great speaking with you. As a confirmation

- I will be there Thursday, the 29th
- at 7:59
- for my 8:03"

Sometimes, the prospect is in the lobby to see if I come in at 7:59. And often, one or two other people are also waiting. Somebody's got my notecard in their hand, and they're holding their watches.

They not only want to see if I show up on time, but they want to get a look at this screwball. And that's okay because the sale has pretty well been set up. They are excited about seeing me because I am out of the ordinary—I have broken out of their expectations. I've brightened their day before they have even met me!

Personalized material highlights your uniqueness. I use about eight different custom notecards. The one at the right is an example.

I have one card that my associates and I did on the com-

The actual notecard size is 5½" × 4¼"; contact information is printed on the back of the card.

puter. We caught the setting Arizona sun in oranges and reds. I'm up on a mountain called Rattlesnake Hill. One that is getting tremendous response is where the whole postcard is my photo on one side with cactus, mountains, and so forth in the background. We just started using these cards. We're getting tons and tons of calls. Most business letters are boring. I don't want my letters to fall into that group!

Keep it coming. One prospect was going to be making a fast decision about who to hire as his speaker for a conference. For a week, we barraged the guy with messages. He got cards; he got a funny bumper sticker. Then I sent a handwritten note. He is from Green Bay and the Packers' team colors are green and yellow. So on the front of the envelope, I took a green highlighter and high-lighted his name. Where it said Green Bay, I used a yellow highlighter. On the back of the envelope , just under the flap, I did two lines, one green and one yellow. I said, "Champs, please open here." He called our office and said, "Tell Bill I love that green and yellow. That's the first time that I've ever gotten anything in our colors."

Leave them with a gift. One consultant who lives in the country takes clients and prospects gifts from his garden. He also has hens that lay brown eggs. These gifts are personal and cre-ative, and not seen as a bribe. He also grows daffodils in front of his office and always takes a bunch on sales calls for the women in the office.

These are just those little extra touches. They're not really much in a way, but few people bother to do them!

A bird in the president's hand is worth... My novel approaches are not the most dramatic I've heard about by any means. In the "Guerrilla Marketing" seminars, they tell the story of a salesperson who had a quarter-million-dollar software setup that his prospect knew would pay for itself quickly and save the company money over the long term. But there was no budget for it and purchasing wouldn't cooperate. After trying to get to the company president, repeatedly and without success, the salesperson sent a carrier pigeon in a box that had to be signed for by the president. The accompanying note said something like, "I've tried every other means of communication to get through to you with a solution your technical people have agreed will save you millions. If you'll name a time and place and tie it to the bird's leg, I'll show up anywhere and buy you lunch." It was so novel, the president had to try it, and the sale was closed.

Dial S for sales. Then there's the salesperson who couldn't get through, so he sent a note with a cellular phone that said "You haven't returned my calls, so here's a phone. All the speed dial numbers are set for me. Please call and I guarantee it will be worth your time." It worked.

* * *

Be yourself—be different. Whatever everybody else is doing—do something else. Don't be part of the boring pack. People buy from a particular salesperson because they like, trust, and respect that person. The first area that I work on is getting them to like me so that the dialogue is open. My being a little bit off the wall—which also makes me more authentic—sets up the relationship.

USE CREATIVITY TO BUILD RELATIONSHIPS

A one-time sale is not usually that big of a deal. True value is in long-term repeat business and referrals. Creativity is important to build relationships and keep them fresh over the years.

At the least, you can be interesting for your customers. But you should also be able to come up with a flow of new ideas that add value for them. Your job in sales is to provide solutions. Most obvious solutions have already been considered. You need to

> ### Marketing For All
> Sales and marketing should involve everyone in the organization. All employees contribute to building creative relationships with customers and prospects. (For instance, see my chapter in *Marketing For People Not In Marketing*.)

use your creativity to offer new possibilities. For instance, I skim 400 trade magazines a month. Often, I find an idea in one industry that can be applied to a client in another industry.

I also try to bring humor to relationships. When I see something funny that might apply to a particular client, my job is to cut it out and stick a little note on it: "Dear Joe, I thought you'd enjoy this." It might be a cartoon—or a funny human interest story that relates to the client's interests.

Creative possibilities spring from the combination of old and new elements. Salespeople are paid to talk to many different people. An alert salesperson has always been like a bee, cross-pollinating ideas among clients and prospects. If you always bring something new when you visit or call, people will be glad to see or hear from you. You bring value—not interruptions—to their busy days.

EAT YOUR WAY TO SUCCESS

The Blades' Breakfast Plan

How would you like to have the time to pick up 250 extra client visits a year? Most people say, "Let's do lunch." Instead, do breakfast! At breakfast, you've got your customers and prospects when they are nice and fresh. You're making your first visit while your competition is still sleeping—or eating alone.

Here's my breakfast master plan. Divide your city up into four quadrants. Find a great restaurant in each quadrant that is easily accessible to clients.

Go to the restaurant the day before your first visit. Ask for the manager—or if it's a mom-and-

---

Instructions to Ensure Great Service

1. Expect Ms. Jones to ask for Bill Blades. Greet her by name.
2. Pour hot tea for her without being asked.
3. Leave us alone for five minutes.
4. Prepare for Ms. Jones to be amazed.

pop operation, ask for the owner. Say, "I'd like to have a couple minutes of your time."

"Sir" or "Ma'am," I say, "I am going to come here tomorrow morning. I've already made a reservation at 7:00 a.m. If you help make this visit really successful, I will come here often. I will bring people who will then bring other people.

"Tomorrow morning, I would like to be seated at that table there in the back. I'd like that to always be Bill's table." At this point, I ask, "Is your best waiter or waitress here today? Someone who's going to be here tomorrow?"

I tell that waitperson, "I've written this down for you. [I hand over the file I've brought with me.] First, tomorrow morning when my guest arrives, I'd like you to say, 'Good morning, Ms. Jones.' [The waitperson will know that a woman asking for me will be Ms. Jones.] Then, "Pour hot tea." [I've already found out in advance through somebody else that this is her favorite beverage.]

Then I tell the restaurant manager or owner, "I have enclosed 25 envelopes addressed to me, postage already affixed. When I finish with a meal, I am always going to get up and walk out of here like I own the joint." Often at restaurant meals, everything is going great until you can't get the blasted check, and it puts a downer on the whole event. You don't want the client sitting there looking at her watch.

I tell the waitperson, "I've already put my American Express number in that file. And there's one last thing I forgot to tell you—I know you'll do

The Group Meal Plan

Here's another creative variation on taking people out for business meals. Instead of taking people out to lunch one at a time, take out a group of noncompeting business people who can benefit from meeting with each other.

You help each individual, you get brownie points for hosting the whole group, and everyone loves the interaction and new contacts.

a great job for me, so here's what I want you to do—always give yourself a 30 percent tip." BOING! What is the difference between a 15 percent tip and a 30 percent tip for two breakfasts? Very little money-wise, but a lot percentage-wise and psychologically.

Treat Them Right

As I keep going back to the same restaurants over and over, I want to make sure that my favorite waiters and waitresses laugh like crazy. I want to make sure they have a good time. I kid around with them a lot. Because they're in a pretty monotonous and mundane position, they get a lot of grumbling: "My food's not done right," etc. So if I'm fun, then I'll get fun and goodwill back. They get 30 percent on top of it. Occasionally, I will come by with baseball tickets. I learn their birthdays. They're astounded. I'm treating them like they should be treating customers. Then I get the same treatment back.

CONCLUSION

Here's a wrap-up story that summarizes the value of creativity in sales. Every week, one salesperson makes a list of important prospects who had refused to see him. One day a week, he makes cold calls on them, taking his potbelly pig with him! He says, "Tell Fred that Bill and his pig are here to see him." Most of the time he gets right in! This exemplifies most of the aspects of creativity in sales: The salesperson gets attention, he's unforgettable, and he creates fun for himself and others.

I'm real big on the value-price relationship. Value has to look like a box that's about 12 inches square so that price looks like a little box that's about 1 inch square.

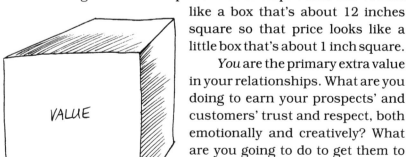

You are the primary extra value in your relationships. What are you doing to earn your prospects' and customers' trust and respect, both emotionally and creatively? What are you going to do to get them to come to you? Your success depends on how much joy and value you provide. If you're not doing anything

creative to blow them right out of their chairs and make them always want to see you, then you are going to find yourself stuck competing on price—and being boring!

Don't be afraid to fail. Don't be afraid to bomb out. Be willing to change yourself to step out of a rut and up to new successes.

ACTION SUMMARY

"It is well to think well; it is divine to act well."
—Horace Mann

- Pick three ideas that fit your style. Do one within a week.

- Make your letters or faxes stand out from the competition. You could design a notecard; start each fax with a quote or humorous saying; use old stamps (purchased at stamp shows) on your envelopes; use envelopes of a distinctive color.

- Come up with at least one costume you could wear to promote your business. (You don't have to wear it yet—just think what it could be. The idea might grow on you.)

- Go over your reading list. Add any publications you don't currently read that would be of interest to prospects and customers.

- Clip relevant cartoons and unusual stories to send to appropriate clients and prospects.

- Start setting your appointments at three or seven minutes after the hour.

- Set up a regular breakfast program at a good restaurant.

- Make a list of gifts you could give customers and prospects. The gifts don't have to be complicated or expensive. They could be from your garden or kitchen. A few chocolate kisses wrapped in a tissue paper square and tied with a ribbon bring smiles (and anticipation of your next visit).

- Ask the most successful salesperson you know to tell you about the most creative technique he or she has ever used.

- Here's a last idea you may be able to adapt. One particular expensive irrigation product pays for itself in water and fertilizer savings in eight months. The salespeople started sending notes eight-months after the sale, saying, "Congratulations, as of today, your system has paid for itself." Could you send quarterly "statements" estimating how much your product or service has saved customers? It's novel and says you care about the value they get.

INDEX

A

Age of Unreason, The (Handy) 106
AIDA marketing formula 146
Alexander, Diane L. 1
Amabile, Teresa 56
American Productivity and Quality Center 32
Amgen, Inc. 6
Analytical thinking 136
Andretti, Mario 118
Anthony, William P. 88, 91
Arnheim, Rudolph 97
Arthur Andersen 32

B

Bacon, Roger 124
Bennett, Robert H. III 88,91
Berg, Deanna H. 103
Blades, Bill 141
Brain
    cell development enhanced by stimulating environment 15
    dominance
        early research 124
        four-quadrant model 22, 124–125
    functions
        left and right brain 12
        split brain theory 12
    structure 12–13
Brainpower
    enhancement of 123–140
    utilizing employees' 10
Brainstorming 55, 65, 67–82
    academic research 75–76
    benefits beyond idea generation 77
    computer-aided 77–78
    example 72–74
    facilitation 69–70
    group vs. individual performance 75
    reversing the problem 79
    rules 68
    solo 70
    specificity of topic 69
    sticky notes on bulletin board 80
    success factors 71–72
    written 79
    visual imagery 101
Breakpoint and Beyond (Land) 42
Breakthrough Thinking (Nadler) 42
Buckler, Sheldon 87
Business meetings at restaurants 151–153

C

Cassidy, Joan 121
Change
    rapid rate 37, 118
    resistance to 33
Cleveland, Grover 101
Coleridge, Samuel Taylor 53
Collaboration as a creativity enhancer 11
Collier, Lindsay 49
Collins, John 146
Communication styles
    effect of supervisor's style on employees 126
Communications Briefings newsletter 10
Community Entrepreneurs Organization 72
Competition to generate ideas 71
Computers
    computer-aided brainstorming 77–78
    used to change business processes 8
Copernicus 59
Corning 11
Costumes as attention-getters 146
Covey, Stephen 41, 111
Crandall, Rick 65
Creative Problem Solver's Toolbox, The (Fobes) 74

Creative Problem Solving
    (Lumsdaine & Lumsdaine) 25
Creative problem-solving 35, 37–50
    model 25–27
Creativity
    from the top down 63
    paradox 9
    subdivision of challenge into
        parts 13
    training programs 19–20
Criticism suspended during
    brainstorming 67, 70, 71
CSC Index Consultants 23
Curiosity
    measuring 63
    teaching 63
Current reality as block to problem
    solving 40
Custom notecards 148–149
Customer service enhanced by use
    of computers 8
Cypress Semiconductor 128

D

de Bono, Edward 44, 46, 81, 118
de Bono's Six Thinking Hats® 46
De Staël, Madame 55
Dendrite development enhanced by
    stimulating environment 15
Diamond, Marian 14
Drucker, Peter 3, 43, 109
Du Pont 74, 93

E

Eastman Kodak 62
Eberle, Bob 78
Edison, Thomas 111
Einstein, Albert 107, 123
Employee suggestions
    Japan vs. U.S. 11
Employees
    ideas valued 10–11
    purpose during Industrial
        Revolution 5
    sharing ideas 10
Encouragement of creativity 27
Enhancing brainpower 121, 123–
    139

Eureka Stimulus Response 44
Executive Edge newsletter 8
Experimental approach to creativ-
    ity 136
Expertise, stifling creativity 108–
    109
Explicit knowledge 20–33

F

Facilitation of brainstorming
    sessions 69–70, 76–77
Facilitators
    impact of increased training on
        brainstorming sessions 76
    necessary competencies 127–
        128
Failure, fear of 6, 107
Failure frame 115
Fame frame 113
Fantasy frame 114
Fear of failure
    stifling creativity 107
Fiction frame 115
Flex frame 110
Flip-side frame 115–116
Forbes magazine 5
Ford, Henry 5
Formula for innovative results
    130
Franklin, Benjamin 16
Free association 77
    brainstorming 68
Freud, Sigmund 63
Friends-and-family frame 112–
    113
FritoLay 95
Fun 63
    brainstorming 68, 71
Fun frame 112
Future frame 110–111

G

Gates, Bill 7
General Electric 10
General Motors 6
Gifts for customers and prospects
    149
Gnosis executives 30

Goethe 67
Gottlieb Duttweiler Foundation 10
Great Game of Business, The (Stack) 112
Greenleaf, Robert 109
Greville 58
Group problem solving participation 46
Growing Up Creative (Amabile) 56
Guided fantasies 114

H

Hall, Doug 44, 71
Handy, Charles 106, 132
Hanks, Kurt 112
Herrmann Brain Dominance Instrument (HBDI) 22, 29, 124–125
Herrmann Model 21, 25
applications of 29
Herrmann, Ned 22, 124–125
Hippocrates 124
Holmes, Oliver Wendell 112
Humor 51, 53–54
personal humor file 60–63
stress inhibitor 59
Huxley, Aldous 56

I

IBM 6
Idea generation
fast-paced process 42
forcing relationships 80
Idea quotas
to increase brainstorming suggestions 76
Ideas
allowing employees to pursue 6
cataloging in database 8
percolation 42–45
sharing of by employees 10
sharing through computer 8
triggered by information 118
Iikubo, Hirotsugu 11

In Search of Excellence (Peters & Waterman) 111
Incentives for increasing suggestions 9
Industrial Revolution
company value determined by labor and physical assets 4
Information sharing 9
Integrated-Brain Technology Model 127, 138
Intellectual capital 1, 3–16
effect on productivity 4
investing in 4
valuing 7
Intellectual Capital (Malone) 7
Intellectual Capital (Stewart) 4
InterDesign 8
Internalization of knowledge 30–31
Interpersonal approach to creativity 137

J

Jackson, John 124
James, William 59, 131
Japanese organizations
orientation towards tacit knowledge 27
Jennings, Eugene 6
JM Huber 9
Journal of Mental Imagery 100
Jump Start Your Brain (Hall) 44, 71
Jung, Carl 85, 86

K

Keener, Charles H. 11
Kekule, August 87
Kennedy, John F. 59
Kiam, Victor 119
Knowledge
explicit 20–33
explicit vs. tacit 19, 27
internalization of 30–31
organizations value of 6
Western organizations vs. Japanese organizations 27

Knowledge-Creating Company, The (Nonaka & Takeuchi) 19, 24
Knowledge creation
  management 32
  model 24–25
    applications 29–32
    operators 27
  process
    hints for managing 26–27
  specialists 27
Kodak 88

L

Land, George 42
Lapp, Janet 111
Lateral thinking 44
Laughter 56–59
Left vs. right brain characteristics 125
Left-brain–right-brain integration 38
Leonard, D. 29
Leonhard Innovation Center for Enhancement of Engineering Education 30
Lichtenberg, George 138
Lowell, James Russell 64
Lumsdaine, Edward 17
Lumsdaine, Monika 17

M

MacKenzie, Gordon 105, 109
Maddox, Nick E. 88, 91
Malone, Michael 7
Management Decisions (Bennett et al.) 91, 97
Managing Beyond the Ordinary (Keener & Iikubo) 11
Mann, Horace 154
Matson, Jack V. 30
Mauzy, Jeffrey 69
McKinney, Joe 39
Memories, Dreams, Reflections (Jung) 86
Mental models
  explicit knowledge 20–33
  prerequisite of organizational innovation 17, 19–34

sharing of, in organizations 20–21
Mental rehearsal 88–90
Mental role playing 87
Michalko, Michael 10, 13, 78
Microsoft Corp. 6
Miller, Henry 97
Mindmapping 80–81
Mindsets
  limiting new ideas 105
Munson, Randall 51

N

National Center on the Educational Quality of the Workforce 4
Nelson, Bob 59
Netscape Communications 7
Netscape Navigator software 7
Newton, Sir Isaac 59
Nin, Anais 107
Nonaka, I. 19, 24

O

Odetics 58
1001 Ways to Energize Employees (Nelson) 59
Opportunity Frame 109
Orbiting the Giant Hairball (MacKenzie) 105
Organization innovation
  sharing of mental models 17, 19–34
Organized approach to problem-solving 137–138
Osborn, Alex 68, 69, 71, 75
Oster, Merrill J. 25

P

Parry, Jay 112
Participation
  group problem solving 46
Pasteur, Louis 59
Patanjali states of visual imagery 86
Percolating ideas 42–50
Perls, Fritz 91, 93
Personalized postage stamps 146

Personalized stationery 148
Perspective future 41–42
Pessimistic outlook
    stifling creativity 108
Peters, Tom 9, 31, 63, 111, 115
Pierce, Jim 35
Planning
    converting ideas to solutions
        47–48
Playing 40–41
Polaroid Corp. 87
Post It Notes® 8
Presentations
    using visualization to improve
        98
Problem solving 35, 37–50
    blocked by current reality 40
    collaborative 46
    creative problem-solving model
        25–27
Product Improvement Checklist
    (PICL) 44
Productivity
    educational level of workers 64
Prospecting for sales leads
    who-is-that-guy approach 145
Psychology of Winning, The
    (Waitley) 90
Purposeful creativity 35, 37–50

R

Ranking ideas 47–48
Rathmann, George 6
Reframing 105–120
    guide 116–117
Relationships with customers and
        prospects
    creativity keeps them fresh
        150–151
    bringing value 144
Relaxation techniques 91–93
Resistance to change 33
Response hierarchies
    free association 77
Retton, Mary Lou 89
Reversing the problem 79
Rewarding creativity 27, 72

Reynolds Metal 7
Richards, Bob 53
Right-brain visualization 100
Risk taking, barriers to 33
Rodgers, T.J. 128
Role playing, mental 87

S

Sales
    creativity in the sales process
        49–161
Sales & Marketing Executive
    Report 144
Sales calls
    adding creative touches 144–
        150
Saxe, J.G. 40
SCAMMPERR technique to
    generate ideas 80
Sears 6
Self-awareness
    enhanced by visual imagery 85
    of mental styles 138
Self-confidence
    increased through visual
        imagery 99–100
Seven Habits of Highly Effective
    People (Covey) 41, 111
Shakespeare, William 110
Sharing ideas 10
    computer database 8
Shaw, George Bernard 85, 114
Sisk, Dorothy A. 83
Six Thinking Hats® 46
Socialization's role in problem
    solving 29
Solo brainstorming 70
Southwest Airlines 112
Sperry, Roger 12
Split-brain theory 12
Springfield Remanufacturing
    Corporation 112
Stack, Jack 112
Steinbeck, John 123
Stephens, Robert 146
Stewart, Thomas 4
Sticky-note brainstorming 80

Stoppard, Tom 115
StoryTime Cards
    visualization tool 45
Straus, S. 29
Stress, inhibited by humor 59
Suggestions
    increasing number by reward-
        ing 10
    increasing number through
        contents 9

T

Tacit knowledge 27
Takeuchi, H. 19, 24
Tasks
    assigning appropriate people
        129
Teams 9, 14
Tesla, Nikola 86–87
Texas Utilities 96
Thinkertoys (Michalko) 12, 13
Thinking
    analytical 142
    enhanced by stimulating
        environment 14–15
Thinking modes 130–131
    appreciation of individual
        differences 131–135
Thinking preferences 21
Thinking styles
    individual differences 23–24
ThinkPak (Michalko) 78
3M Corp. 6
Time-track visualization 100
Training
    enhancing visualization ability
        100
    resistance to 96–97
    visual imagery 90–97
Training programs 19–20
    improvement through use of
        mental models 28–32
Transformation Thinking (Wycoff)
    64
Turner Broadcasting 146

Turner, Ted 146
Twain, Mark 81
Tyler Corp. 39

U

University of California Berkeley
    14
Unspoken assumptions hindering
    new ideas 43

V

Value-price relationship 153
VanGundy, Arthur 44
Visual imagery 85–102
    accessing unconscious 85
    history 86–87
    mental role playing 87
    training 90–97
    used to increase self-confidence
        99–100
Visual mapping 39
Visualization
    benefits 91
    keys to success 100
    of future 41–42
    random word stimuli 44
    time-track 100

W

Wabash National Corporation 8
Waitley, Denis 90
Wake Up Your Creative Genius
    (Hanks & Parry) 112
Waterman, Michael 111
Wecker, David 71
Welch, Jack 10
Western New York Futurists 49
Wheatley, Margaret 105
Wheatley, Walter J. 88, 91
Who-is-that-guy approach to
    prospecting 145–146
Wright, Orville 59
Wright, Wilbur 59
Wycoff, Joyce 64

RECOMMENDED READINGS AND RESOURCES

Readings

Amabile, Teresa M. (1989). *Growing Up Creative.* New York: Crown.

Arthur Andersen and Company. (1995). *Highlights of the Knowledge Imperative Symposium.* Chicago: Arthur Andersen & Co., pp. 10-11.

Ayan, Jordan. (1996). *Aha! 10 Ways to Free Your Creative Spirit and Find Your Great Ideas.* New York: Random House.

Blades, Bill. (1998, in press). "Servant Selling." In R. Crandall (Ed.), *Marketing for People Not in Marketing.* Corte Madera: Select Press.

Bolman, Lee G., & Deal, Terrence E. (1991). *Reframing Organizations.* San Francisco: Jossey-Bass.

Cytowic, Richard. (1993). *The Man Who Tasted Ships.* New York: Putnam.

Diamond, Marian. (1988). Enriching Heredity: The Impact of the Environment on the Anatomy. New York: Macmillan.

Drucker, Peter. (1993, October 21). "The Five Deadly Business Sins." *The Wall Street Journal.*

Edvinsson, Leif, & Malone, Michael S. (1996). *Intellectual Capital: Realizing Your Company's True Value by Finding Its Hidden Brainpower.* New York: Harper Business.

Fobes, Richard. (1993). *The Creative Problem Solver's Toolbox.* Corvallis, OR: Solutions Through Innovation.

Foster-Harrison, E.S. (1994). *More Energizing Icebreakers for All Ages and Stages* (Book 2). Memphis, TN: Educational Media.

Gawain, Shakti. (1982). *Creative Visualization.* New York: Bantam New Age Books.

Hall, Doug. (1995). *Jump Start Your Brain.* New York: Warner Books.

Handy, Charles. (1989). *The Age of Unreason.* Boston: Harvard Business School Press.

Hanks, Kurt, & Parry, Jay. (1992). *Wake Up Your Creative Genius.* Menlo Park, CA: Crisp Publications.

Herrmann, Ned. (1989). *The Creative Brain.* Lake Lure, NC: Brain Books.

Herrmann, Ned. (1996). *The Whole-Brain Business Book.* New York: McGraw-Hill.

Houghton, James R. (1994, November). "Global Competition: Unleashing the Power of People." Remarks to the Cornell Corporate Forum, Cornell University, Ithaca, New York.

Jaffe, Dennis. (1986). *Healing From Within*. New York: Simon & Schuster.

Kepner, Charles H., & Iikubo, Hirotsugu. (1996). *Managing Beyond the Ordinary: Using Collaboration to Solve Problems, Make Decisions & Achieve Extraordinary Results*. New York: AMACOM.

Leonard, Dorothy, & Straus, Susan. (1997). "Putting Your Company's Whole Brain to Work." *Harvard Business Review*, July–August, 111–121, Reprint 97407.

Lumsdaine, Edward, & Lumsdaine, Monika. (1994). *Creative Problem Solving: Thinking Skills for a Changing World*. New York: McGraw Hill.

MacKenzie, Gordon. (1996). *Orbiting the Giant Hairball*. Shawnee Mission, KS: OpusPocus Publishing.

Michalko, Michael. (1990). *Thinkertoys: A Handbook of Creativity in Business*. Berkeley, CA: Ten Speed Press.

Nadler, Gerald, & Hibino, Shozo. (1989). *Breakthrough Thinking: Why We Must Change the Way We Solve Problems*. Rocklin, CA: Prima Publications.

National Center on the Educational Quality of the Workforce. (1995). "The Other Shoe: Education's Contribution to the Productivity of Establishments." Philadelphia: University of Pennsylvania.

Nonaka, Ikujiro, & Takeuchi, Hirotaka. (1995). *The Knowledge-Creating Company*. New York: Oxford University Press.

Perls, Fritz. (1958, June). *Gestalt Techniques*. Esalen Workshop, June 7–10, Big Sur, California.

Siau, Keng L. (1995). Group Creativity and Technology. *Journal of Creative Behavior, 29*, 201–216.

Schwarz, Peter. (1991). *The Art of the Long View*. New York: Doubleday/Currency.

Sisk, D., & Shallcross, D. (1986). *Leadership: Making Things Happen*. Buffalo, New York: Bearly Limited.

Sisk, D., & Shallcross, D. (1989). *Intuition: An Inner Way of Knowing*. Buffalo, New York: Bearly Limited.

Stack, Jack. (1992). *The Great Game of Business*. New York: Currency Books.

Stewart, Thomas A. (1997). *Intellectual Capital: How the Knowledge Economy is Creating New Challenges for Corporations & New Opportunities for the People Who Work for Them*. New York: Doubleday.

Wycoff, Joyce. (1995). *Transformation Thinking*. New York: Berkley Publications.

Resources

American Creativity Association
P.O. Box 2029
Wilmington, DE 19899-2029
(302) 239-7673
e-mail ACA Moyer@aol.com

Centers for Studies in Creativity
Buffalo State College
1300 Elmwood Ave., Chase Hall 244
Buffalo, NY 14222-1095
(716) 878-6223
(716) 878-4040 fax
www.BuffaloState.edu/creative/cschp.html

The Creative Education Foundation (CEF)
1050 Union Rd.
Buffalo, NY, 14224
(716) 675-3181

Creative Thinking Association of America
1600 Sprague Rd., Suite #120
Cleveland, OH, 44130
(440) 243-5576
(440) 243-8754 fax
e-mail thinkcta@aol.com
http://members.aol.com/vancecta/web/cta.htm

Innovation Network
34 E. Sola St., Suite D-11
Santa Barbara, CA 93101
(805) 965-8477
(805) 963-8220 fax
e-mail Joyce@thinksmart.com
www.thinksmart.com

Inventure Place
National Inventors Hall of Fame
221 South Broadway St.
Akron, OH 44308-1505
(330) 762-4463
(330) 762-6313 fax
www.nforce.com/projects/inventure/inventure.html

The National Center for Creativity, Inc.
2728 Maynard Dr.
Indianapolis, IN 46227
(317) 639-6224
(800) 306-6224
(317) 639-6225 fax
http://indyunix.iupui.edu/~ncci/ncci.html

US Patent and Trademark Office
Washington, DC 20231
(703) 308-4357